Hebrews

HEBREWS

CHALLENGES TO
BOLD DISCIPLESHIP

Herschel H. Hobbs

Broadman Press
Nashville, Tennessee

4213–23
ISBN: 0–8054–1323–5

Dewey Decimal Classification: 227.87
Subject headings: BIBLE—NEW TESTAMENT—HEBREWS

Library of Congress Catalog Card Number: 74–178062
Printed in the United States of America

Previously published as *How to Follow Jesus*

DEDICATED TO
Christian missionaries
who are filling their
place in God's redemptive
world-mission.

Contents

Introduction

In 1954 the author's little book *Studies in Hebrews* was published and many said that it presented a new approach to the meaning and purpose of the book of Hebrews. Its scope permitted only a sketchy treatment of the main ideas. Beginning then and continuing through the years many have expressed the hope that a more complete work along these suggested lines might be produced. During this intervening time the author has continued to study the book in view of such an attempt, and this work is the fruit of that effort.

This volume grew out of a sense of inadequacy of the more traditional views of *Hebrews*. These will be pointed out shortly. As the author read this unique New Testament book in various translations and studied it from the Greek text, there came a growing conviction that its purpose was related to *the world-mission of Christianity*. After completing the first draft of the 1954 work, the author read William Manson's *The Epistle to the Hebrews*.[1] He was gratified that so able a scholar held to the same basic idea, though he had developed it along different lines. It is these differences which seem to merit this present work. But this writer shares with Dr. Manson as he expresses his hopes. "If my construction of the facts is disallowed, I shall look to be refuted; if it is defective, I trust that it will be improved; if it should be thought right, I hope that even within its limits it may help at certain important points to put Christian doctrine more squarely on the foundation of Christian history" (pp. vii f.).

Before dealing with the text itself certain matters need attention. These have to do with elements which throw light upon the text.

We believe that Hebrews should be viewed, not in isolation, but as a part of God's eternal purpose of redemption. This purpose like a mighty healing stream finds its source eternally in the heart of God, which beats with redemptive love. Forgiveness was in the heart of God before sin was in the heart of man. Thus, Christ is the Lamb slain before the creation of the universe. God's redeeming purpose is seen even in the tragic shades of Eden (Gen. 3:15). This *underground* stream emerged historically in God's covenant with Abraham (Gen. 12:1 ff.). It broadened into the channel of God's covenant people Israel (Ex. 19:1 ff.) but became a river temporarily delayed in the dry sands of a disobedient people. Even in Israel's darkest days it was the theme of many of the prophets. But in Jesus Christ it burst forth as a fountain of living water whose flow is the river of the water of life to the nations. And this writer believes that Hebrews was written to send this river on its way to become a mighty ocean lapping the shores of every continent and of the isles of the seven seas.

As Hebrews is important, it is also fraught with problems for its interpreters. No other New Testament book presents more unsolved problems. But its importance makes it all the more necessary that the problems should be noted. While there exists a consensus that Hebrews is genuine Scripture, there is by no means agreement for solving its problems. It is proposed, therefore, to examine the more salient ones.

1. The Matter of Title and Style

Someone suggested that every word in the familiar title of the King James Version, "The Epistle of Paul the Apostle to the Hebrews," has been challenged by present-day scholarship. Certainly this title does not appear in the oldest and best manuscripts. It was probably written by some copyist after the work became widely associated with the apostle's name.

The most ancient manuscripts carry the title "To Hebrews." Even this is questioned as to its originality by some scholars, but on the basis of present manuscript evidence it may be accepted. Even those who agree on this title, however, find problems as to whether "Hebrews" refers to non-Christian or Christian Hebrews.

As for style someone has noted that Hebrews fits into no one category. It begins like an *essay,* proceeds like a *sermon,* and ends like a *letter.* While this is true, it is evident that the greatest portion is definitely sermonic in form. Frederick C. Grant sees it as a homily, sermon, or address. He points out that even the opening verses follow the ancient Greek form of oratory.

> The opening paragraph of Hebrews is a grand rhetorical overture, proclaiming the theme as with full orchestra, and alliteration, rhythm, emphatic order of words, balance and climax. No epistle in the New Testament begins in this way, and none displays such consummate literary skill . . . The periodic structure of the sentences and their almost rhythmic pattern show that the author was also skilled in the arts of the Hellenistic rhetorician.[2]

The author's use of language shows throughout that he was skilled in the *Koine* Greek.

2. The Question of Authorship

Perhaps in no other matter is there a wider difference of opinion. And *opinion* is the word for it, because the book itself makes no statement as to its author. It has been variously assigned to Paul, Barnabas, Apollos, Peter, Luke, Timothy (despite 13:23), Priscilla, Silas, Philip, Aristion, and Clement of Rome. Certainly Priscilla can be eliminated since the author refers to himself with a masculine pronoun. Perhaps the three most seriously considered are the first three.

Martin Luther suggested Apollos, and he is followed by many modern scholars. The picture of Apollos in Acts lends strength to this theory. Tertullian first proposed Barnabas as the author.

The same arguments from the book itself may apply to either of these. Both were related to the Alexandrian school of thought which is evident in Hebrews. Both would have been familiar with the Septuagint (Greek translation of the Old Testament), which is quoted in the book. Apollos was certainly a great preacher, and Barnabas was called the son of exhortation. It is likely that both men were familiar with the levitical laws of sacrifice, either personally or from their knowledge of the Scriptures.

Grant suggests that the author may not necessarily have been a Jew himself (a position which this writer questions), "and probably never attended a service of sacrificial worship in the temple at Jerusalem. In fact, his views of sacrifice are derived exclusively from the written Pentateuch. . . . The Jewish worship with which he is familiar took place in the 'tent' or 'tabernacle' in the wilderness, not in the Herodian temple at Jerusalem." [3]

This may or may not be true. If true, it could argue against Barnabas. But this writer sees another reason for referring to the tabernacle rather than to the temple. His entire argument centers in the *Exodus epic* (see section 5) long before even Solomon's temple was built.

Despite the widespread tradition that sees Paul as the author, in all likelihood he is one of the least probable ones. For one thing, the author in 2:2 speaks of himself as belonging to that generation of Christians which had not personally seen the Lord Jesus but who received the gospel from those who heard it from him. In writings which are Pauline without question Paul insists that he had seen the Lord (cf. 1 Cor. 9:1) and that he received his message by direct revelation (cf. Gal. 1:12). Furthermore, it is difficult to see Paul writing such a book, especially to Hebrew Christians. It was out of such a group in Jerusalem that the Judaizers came to perplex Paul and to deny his apostolic authority. Also Gleason Archer, Jr., notes, "There are such differences in style and logical approach as to indicate very strongly a different author; Paul never employs the cultivated, literary diction and rhetorical polish which sets *Hebrews* in marked contrast to all of the other N.T. books." [4]

In the writer's class notes dating from seminary days are ten reasons given by W. Hersey Davis as evidence against the Pauline authorship of Hebrews:

(1) The covenant spoken of is the covenant of Sinai. No mention is made of the covenant with Abraham or of circumcision as a sign of that covenant. The atonement is presented not in its judicial aspects, but as a removing of sin or dead works which had interrupted communion with God.

(2) Sin is not considered as a transgression of the moral law, but as a defilement which is a disqualification for moral worship.

(3) The dispensation discussed is not a code of laws but a system of worship.

(4) The gospel is not presented as antagonistic to the Mosaic law, but as the natural climax to the Mosaic revelation and the true key to its interpretation.

(5) Christianity is the true flower or final development of Judaism.

(6) Redemption is not treated as the reconciliation of enemies, but as the cleansing of God's children from pollution. The "children" are already in the covenant of God. (Not Jews as such, but those who have believed in Christ.)

(7) The word "purify" does not refer to moral cleansing, but to the "gift."

(8) "To sanctify" is to place the people in the relation of worshippers to (and servants of) God.

(9) To "perfect" and to "complete" do not refer to moral purification, but mean "to bring to appropriate ends objectively" (2:10). This verse refers to carrying his mission through to the appropriate end by suffering. It is an objective end, not a subjective one. The writer is speaking to holy people *(hagios).*

(10) The object of the epistle seems to be to prevent the apostasy of the Christian Jews. The argument used is that the Christian dispensation is the final and perfect one, just as the old dispensation was temporary and incomplete and preparatory.

The writer agrees with most of these items. The major exception is Number 10. But even here one must define "apostasy" (see 3:12). The "argument" is true, but the application of it admits various positions. Note that Dr. Davis said *seems.* He was not dogmatic.

Furthermore, some of the things included in this list may be applied to Paul. However, the overall seems to argue against him as the author.

One man's *guess* is as good as another's. If the writer had to make a *guess* he would choose Barnabas. But Apollos would be just as intelligent a guess. Only Origen has made a definitive statement as to the authorship of Hebrews. And that is that "only God knows."

3. The Problem of Date

This is another widely disputed matter. Some would date its writing in the period A.D. 81–94. Others see it as being somewhere between A.D. 50–70. Certainly it cannot be dated later than A.D. 95. For Clement of Rome made use of Hebrews in his letter to Corinth.

Some argue for the later date on the basis that its readers had been converted through the efforts of the Lord's personal disciples. However, this condition, especially outside of Palestine, could fit any date following the spread of the gospel beyond that land. It is suggested that the doctrinal content falls within a period between the later Pauline epistles (e.g. Colossians, about A.D. 63) and the Johannine epistles (A.D. 80–95). It could fit the early part of this period. If the *world-mission* idea be accepted it could fall within the approximate time of 1 Peter (*ca.* A.D. 65–67; cf. 1 Peter 2:9–10).

The readers of the epistle are said to have endured persecution (10:33 ff.; 12:4). This could be either the one under Nero (A.D. 64–68) or the one under Domitian (A.D. 81–82). It could refer to some local situation. But assuming one of the others, the degree of persecution suggests the former.

Timothy's release could be a clue as to the date. Probably he was imprisoned when he went to Rome at Paul's request (2 Tim. 4:11–13, 21). If so, he may have been released sometime after Nero's death, June 8, A.D. 68. But if one holds that the letter was sent *to* Rome, this perhaps refers to some other imprisonment. However, it would be less likely to refer to one too far beyond that time.

Many hold that the fall of Jerusalem (A.D. 70) is a focal point in dating Hebrews. The author does not mention this event, which would certainly have strengthened his argument. But he does infer that some impending event would mean that the temple and its sacrificial system still in existence (10:1 ff.) were "ready to vanish away" (8:13). The Jewish War lasted from A.D. 66 to 70. It is possible that Hebrews was written late in this period when events heralded the end of the temple and its system, e.g. A.D. 68–69.

It is evident, therefore, that the terminal dates are about A.D. 48 and 95. The internal evidence does not require a time later than thirty or forty years after Pentecost or A.D. 60–70. Such a time brings us to the period of the Neronic persecution. The temple in Jerusalem was still standing but was ready to pass away. This occurred in A.D. 70, which could mean that Hebrews was probably written about A.D. 69.

4. The Question as to Destination

To whom was Hebrews written? Through the years various places have had their champions: Jerusalem, Palestine, Antioch, Alexandria, Rome, Colossae, Ephesus, Berea, and even Ravenna. Grant notes certain late manuscripts which mention that it was written from Rome, Italy, or Athens. But he calls them "mere guesses of later copyists." However, this does suggest lack of certainty about the matter.

Until the nineteenth century Palestine or Jerusalem was generally accepted as the destination. But certain matters make this improbable, especially Jerusalem. It could hardly be said that the Christians there had all received the gospel secondhand (2:3). Also while they may have suffered loss of property (10:32 ff.), they certainly had those among them who had resisted unto blood, Stephen and James the apostle (12:4).

The most probable recipient would seem to be either Alexandria or Rome. The allegorical style of the epistle would be understood in Alexandria. The case for Rome rests on one's understanding of "they of Italy" (13:24). Was the epistle written from Italy to Alexandria or some other place? Or was it written from one of these places to Italy or Rome? In the Greek text the preposition is *apo*, away from. This suggests those *from* Italy who lived elsewhere. The preposition *ek*, out of, would more likely have referred to people living in Italy. On this basis it may be that the letter was addressed to those living in Rome. The matter of Timothy's release poses a problem, but as seen previously it could be explained otherwise. In view of the world-mission idea, Rome would be a more likely place.

All that can be said with any degree of certainty is that it was written from some place in the Roman Empire to a local congregation of Hebrew Christians located elsewhere in the empire. There are those, however, that question the Hebrew-Christian idea. Some hold that it was written to non-Christian Hebrews, while others question "To Hebrews" and see its recipients as Christians of

Gentile extraction. This latter view dates from E. M. Röth in 1836.[5] However, the contents of the letter favor Hebrew Christians as the addressees.

Fortunately, the lack of knowledge as to the destination of Hebrews does not detract from its validity and message. This uncertainty even enhances the universal nature of its message.

5. The Problem of Purpose

This is the heart of the matter. For one's understanding as to its purpose will greatly color one's interpretation of Hebrews.

One school of thought sees its purpose as a warning to Jews contemplating becoming Christians not to stop short of receiving Christ as Savior. However, the language favors the readers as being Christians.

As noted previously one position is that the epistle was written to Gentile Christians who were tempted to return to pagan ways. But again the Hebrew element of the epistle seems to deny this.

The oldest and most widely held view is that the purpose is to warn Hebrew Christians not to forsake Christ and return to Judaism. Thus, the new covenant is pictured as superior in every way to the old covenant. It should be noted, however, that "apostasy" (3:12, *apostēnai*), regardless of how one may define the word, is not toward Judaism but "from the living God." So the issue is much broader and deeper than this.

A more recent suggestion is that the problem faced by the readers was not that of returning to Judaism, but a state of arrested development as they continued to dwell under the shadow of Judaism.[6] Akin to this is the view that they had not progressed beyond the elementary stages of Christian truth, so were challenged to go further toward a full knowledge of Christ and the gospel.[7] Certainly the writer agrees with Thomas' idea that the key thought in the epistle is "Let us go on" (6:1). But go on to what? And we agree with Manson that not enough emphasis has been placed on the eschatological tone of the epistle.[8] This note of urgency runs throughout. But again the question persists as to what it is that should be done so urgently.

Which brings us to the writer's understanding of the purpose of Hebrews. Certainly he is reluctant to challenge the positions of able scholars through the years. However, his position is somewhat akin to the general ideas presented by Manson and Thomas. The theme is not "Don't go back!" but "Let us go on!" The difference lies in that toward which the readers are to move. But with this question pending let us look at the more traditional position.

In the writer's judgment interpreters have magnified the author's arguments to the neglect of his main thesis. To be sure, Hebrews presents one of the most exalted pictures of Christ found in the New Testament. But the author's purpose was not primarily to deal in Christology. And as will be seen later he was not warning against *apostasy* in the modern sense of the word. Such a position presupposes the possibility of a loss of one's personal salvation. The New Testament abundantly teaches otherwise (cf. John 3:16, 18; 10:28 f.; Eph. 1:13–14;

2:8–10; Col. 3:3).

Too often the word "salvation" is read with one thought in mind, regeneration or justification. But the word is also used of sanctification and glorification. In Hebrews the author assumes a justified people. So his emphasis is upon *sanctification* (2:1–3) and *glorification* (9:28).

Hebrews is basically a sermon. In form and style the author is skilled in homiletics. For this reason it appears that we should look for his purpose not in his *argument* but in his *application* or *exhortation* (cf. 2:1 ff.; 3:7 ff.; 6:1 ff.; 10:19 ff.; 12:1 ff.). What is he trying to get his readers to do about the truth presented? He wants them to move from where they are in their Christian experience to where God wills them to be. He has called them for a purpose. And they are to fulfil that purpose. This purpose has to do with God's world-mission in redemption for all men.

Manson uses the term "world-mission." But he relates it back to Stephen's speech in Acts 7. Following a recitation of Hebrew history, Stephen charged his listeners with being a people "stiff-necked and uncircumcised in heart and ears" who always resist the Holy Spirit. But his words were directed primarily at their rejection of Jesus as the Christ. The theme of Acts 7 is that through the ages God presented his servant, men rejected him, but God authenticated him (cf. Acts 7:9–10, 17–21, 27–36, 51–53). This principle he also applied to Jesus (vv. 55 f.) The greater purpose of Christ's coming was involved, of course, but it is seen in Stephen's speech only by implication.

In all likelihood the author of Hebrews was familiar with the story about Stephen. He could even have read it from Acts itself. But it is even more certain that he was familiar with God's redemptive purpose through the covenant people Israel. Like Paul (Rom. 9 f.) and Peter (1 Peter 2:4–10) he saw the Christian people as the true Israel of God. It was through them that God's redemptive purpose in Christ was to be propagated. And to what better group could he declare this than to a small Hebrew-Christian congregation?

The group to which he wrote, like so many Christians today, was content to be redeemed from the bondage of sin. They had not caught the larger vision of growing and serving in the fuller salvation of *sanctification.* Thus they were in danger of losing the full-salvation of *glorification,* not heaven itself, but the sum-total of glory and reward in heaven.

It was against this background that he used the allegorical method of interpretation to challenge them to move out in their world-mission of evangelizing the world. This allegorical method he applied to the Exodus epic of ancient Israel. He pointed to Israel's failure under the old covenant with Moses, and warned his readers that they should not suffer the same failure under the new covenant which centered in Christ. The superior covenant involved greater responsibility. And failure in it entailed greater penalty; not the loss of redemption but the loss of opportunity as a redeemed people.

Thus the author's exhortations had nothing to do with apostasy back into Judaism or a loss of redemption. They were challenges to go on in the fulfilment of their divinely given mission—to be a people of evangelism and missions. Thus this book did not speak merely to an ancient people about a problem of their time alone. It speaks to the followers of Christ in every age. It is a call to world-mission today.

Notes

1. Hodder and Stoughton, Ltd., London, 1951.
2. *The Epistle to the Hebrews* (Annotated Bible Series), Harper, New York, 1956, p. 5.
3. *Ibid.*, p. 6.
4. *The Epistle to the Hebrews,* Baker, Grand Rapids, 1957, p. 4.
5. Manson, *op. cit.,* p. 16. See section 5 on both of these positions.
6. See Manson, *op. cit.,* p. 24, "V."
7. W. H. Griffith Thomas, *Let Us Go On,* Zondervan, Grand Rapids, 1944, pp. 10 f.
8. *Op. cit.,* p. 9.

I. The Supreme Revelation

One of the key words in Hebrews is "better." Everything about the Christian message is better than that contained in the Old Testament. It is upon this basis that the author repeatedly challenged his readers to faithfulness in God's redemptive world-mission. His first declaration was that the Christian revelation is better than that which preceded it. Indeed, it is the supreme revelation of God to man.

1. The Previous Revelation (1:1)

God, who at sundry times and in divers manners spake in time past unto the fathers by the prophets.

A better or supreme revelation must have that with which it may be compared. In the Greek text the greater emphasis is placed upon the manner of the previous revelation. The secondary emphasis is upon the means through which the revelation was given. Thus verse 1 begins with *polumerōs kai polutropōs, many portions* or measures and *many ways.* It ends with *en tois prophētais,* in the sphere of the prophets.

The Old Testament revelation was progressive. It came in different times and ways. Any given part was incomplete without the whole. And it was given to men in the sphere of the prophets or those who spoke forth for God.

But in all of these it was God speaking. He spoke "of old time" *(palai)* or long ago. In this verse "spake" is an aorist participle. The aorist tense regards the speaking as a whole. And the participle *(lalēsas)* suggests the incompleteness of the old revelation. It was given **to the fathers,** the ancestors of the readers of this epistle, at various times and in terms that they could understand. But always it was a gradual unfolding of God's redemptive will and purpose.

It is clear, therefore, that the revelation was not confined to the so-called major and minor prophets. Certainly in the author's mind there were God's words spoken at intervals to Abraham about his redemptive purpose (cf. Gen. 12:1 ff.), and to Moses as he prepared a people through whom his purpose should run. However, it was not confined to these men. As one turns the pages of the Old Testament on each page he finds the gradual and increasing unveiling of God's will.

2. The Full Revelation (1:2a)

Hath in these last days spoken unto us by his Son. Here the primary emphasis is upon **these last days** or the period of the incarnation. Coming at the end of the statement, **Son** occupies the place of second emphasis, corresponding to the place of the prophets in the old revelation. Here the verb "hath spoken" renders an aorist indicative form, third person singular. In contrast to the participle in verse 1 it means a final, complete speaking. So a full revelation. And it is "in the sphere of [*en*] Son." There is no definite article before Son. It means one who bears the relation to God of Son.

In the Greek text the author presented a balance in contrast between verses 1 and 2*a*. Over against "many portions and many ways of old time" he placed "upon the last of these days." And across from "in the sphere of the prophets" he placed "in the sphere of Son." He contrasted partial "speaking" with the complete "spake." And God is the speaker in both cases. In the former God spoke to the fathers. In the latter He spoke to us.

Westcott gives a striking analysis of these verses:

The contrast between the Old Revelation and the New is marked in three particulars. There is a contrast (a) in the method, and (b) in the time, and (c) in the agents of the two revelations.

(a) The earlier teaching was conveyed in successive portions and in varying fashions according to the needs and capacities of those who received it: on the other hand the revelation in Him who was Son was necessarily complete in itself (comp. John 1:14, 18).

(b) The former revelation was given *of old time,* in the infancy and growth of the world: the Christian revelation *at the end of these days,* on the very verge of the new order which it necessarily ushered in.

(c) The messengers in whom God spoke before, were the long line of prophets raised from age to age *since the world began* (Lk. 1:70; Acts 3:21): the Messenger of the new dispensation was God's own Son.[1]

Thus God is the source of all truth which he reveals in his own times, ways, and means. The incarnation of his Son is the center of all life. He is Truth. And God's full, final revelation to man is in and through him. While the Greek verbs for speaking, *laleō,* here and *legō,* related to *logos,* are different, one cannot fail to see a kinship in thought in the opening verses of Hebrews and those of John's Gospel where Christ is presented as the *Logos.* He is the open, spoken manifestation of God to men. God's partial speaking through the prophets evolved into his final, complete speaking through the *Logos.* And while the Holy Spirit continues to lead into a greater understanding of the Son (John 16:13–14), God has spoken completely and finally in him.

3. The Nature and Role of the Son (1:2b–4)

Having placed the Son in the center of the stage, the author described him in both his nature and his role in redemptive history. Comparison here should be made with John 1:1–18 and Colossians 1:15–20; 2:9. Both John and Paul were answering the philosophy of the Gnostics. It would seem that this author was doing the same. No doubt his readers were confronted with this philosophy which sought to deprive Jesus Christ of full deity.

By a series of personal pronouns (whom, whom, who) the author dealt with the Son. Westcott notes that God is the subject of the verbs in verses 1–2 and Son is the subject of the verbs in verses 3–4.

Whom he hath appointed heir of all things (v.2b). The idea of Sonship moves naturally to that of Heirship (cf. Rom. 8:17). God has *placed* (timeless aorist form of *tithēmi*) the Son in the position of *heir.* There never was a time when this was not true. "All things" renders *pantōn* without the definite article. This refers to every single part of the universe from atoms to solar systems. This also included the spiritual universe. There is nothing of which the Son is not the heir, either natural or spiritual.

By whom also he made the worlds (v.2c). "By" renders *dia,* through. God's creative activity was through the Son as the intermediate Agent (cf. Jn. 1:3; Col. 1:16). Note God's spoken word *(Logos),* "And God said" (Gen. 1:3, 6, 9, 11, 14, 20, 24, 26, 29). **The worlds** translates *tous aiōnas,* the ages. This includes everything in both time and space. It may be understood as the *cosmos* (Heb. 11:3) or "the all things" *(ta panta,* v.3). John 1:3 reads, "Every single part of the universe [*panta* without the article] through him come into being." Colossians 1:16 reads, "In the sphere of him was created the universe as a whole" *(ta panta).*

Who being the brightness of his glory, and the express image of his person, and upholding all things by the word of his power (v.3a).

Being renders *eimi,* expressing essential being. He did not *become (ginomai,* v. 4) but always has been the **brightness** or effulgence of the glory. This brightness *(apaugasma)* may be either the reflected glory of the Father (Calvin, Thayer) or the essential glory of the Son himself. It more likely is the latter. The Greek word basically means a ray of light from an original light body.[2] Of course, Christ revealed the Father. But this glory was resident in him also as a Person of the Godhead (cf. Matt. 17:1 ff.). "The glory," not *"his* glory," may refer to God's glory seen in Jesus Christ. Or it may refer to the glory resident in Jesus himself. In either case he was the Shekinah Glory dwelling among men (Jn. 1:14).

The Son is also **the express image** *(charaktēr,* note "character") of God's "person" or substance. *Charaktēr* is from *charassō,* to cut, scratch, or mark. It first denoted the tool used in such. But later it came to mean the result. The figure is that of the exact reproduction as of the printing of a form. The word was also used for "character." So the Son is exactly like the Father. As he said, "I and my Father are one" (John 10:30).

The word rendered **person** is *hupostaseōs* referring to the very essence of God. Its meaning is expressed in Colossians 2:9. Literally, "For in him alone permanently abides all the essence of deity, the state of being God in bodily form." The author of Hebrews clearly set forth the essential deity of the Son.

But what is the Son's relation to the universe? Not only is he the Creator or

Heir of the universe. He also is **upholding all things by the word of his power** (v.3a). The idea is that he is *bearing (pherōn)* "the all things" or universe as a whole. And he does so "by the word [*rhemati*] of his power." The thought is the expression of his power.

Westcott notes that bearing should not be regarded merely as supporting a dead weight.[3] It is more that of carrying forward the universe, both natural and spiritual, toward its intended goal. Again this is a reminder of Colossians 1: 16–17. "The universe as a whole through him and unto him stands created . . . And the universe in him holds together."

But the Son also bears a redemptive relation to man, and is the ruler over all things, both natural and spiritual.

When he had . . . purged our sins, sat down on the right hand of the Majesty on high (v.3b). "By himself" is not in the best manuscripts, but the idea is true. However, this thought is present in the aorist middle participle *poiēsamenos,* "having made in himself." In his death he performed the one act of purging or purification of sins. Here is a reference to his priestly work treated more fully later in the epistle (7:24 ff.; 9:7–28). In the best texts "our" is absent. But in his atoning work the Son provided cleansing from all sin, including *ours.*

And having done so, he **sat down** (took his seat, aorist) on the right hand, the position of greatest power and dignity, of the Majesty or God in his greatness in heaven. The picture is that of dignity, power, and majesty (cf. John 17:5; 1 Cor. 15:25; Phil. 2:9–11). This thought anticipates 10:12–13.

The picture is that of the Son reigning in his mediatorial kingdom. In it he is bringing all things under his rule in both the natural and spiritual universe. Each time one soul surrenders to him it is subdued unto himself. This thought involves the world-mission to which his people are called.

Of interest is the fact that in verses 2–3 the Son is presented as *Prophet* (God spoke through Him), *Priest* (himself purged), and King (sat down). This three-fold picture is seen as basic in the thought of this epistle.

Being made so much better than the angels, as he hath by inheritance obtained a more excellent name than they (v.4).

The climax to the author's description of the Son sees him as "so much better than the angels becoming." This is the first in a series showing that the new covenant in Christ is superior to the old covenant. The key to this idea is "becoming." It renders the verb *ginomai,* not essential being but that which one becomes. Of course, the Son is essentially greater than angels, messengers, or servants. But his "becoming" suggests that the divine Son *became* what he had not been before. Prior to his incarnation he was the divine *Creator.* When he returned to heaven he did so as the *Human-Divine Creator-Redeemer.* This is the "highly exalted" of Philippians 2:9. It is the glory beyond his previous glory prior to the incarnation. Angels are but servants (Heb. 1:14). He is the Saviour.

His **more excellent name** suggests Philippians 2:9–11. The "name which is above every name" is Jesus, "Jehovah is salvation." "Jesus Christ is Lord" means that this Human-Divine One is Jehovah acting in redemption. Before such a "name" the word "angel" pales into insignificance.

Truly, the author exhausted human language in seven (perfect number) figures describing the glory of the Son. He is Heir of the universe (v.2b), Creator of the universe (v.2c), full-revelation of God (v.3a), Sustainer of the universe (v.3b), Redeemer from sins (v.3c), reigning King (v.3d), and superior to angels (v.4).

This comparison of the Son with angels is also related to God's revelation. The Jews regarded the Mosaic law as being given through angels (cf. Acts 7:38, 53). So as the Son is superior to angels, also God's revelation through him is superior to that given through *angels* to Moses.

4. Scriptural Proof of the Son's Superiority (1:5–13)

Having asserted that the Son is superior to angels, the author proceeded to support it from the Old Testament Scriptures. He cited seven passages to this effect. Note the perfect number again. As a class angels were called sons of God. This is probably the meaning of Job 38:7. But it was a far different thought from that in the author's mind. The first reference was to Psalm 2:7.

For unto which of the angels said he at any time, Thou art my Son, this day have I begotten thee? (v.5a). God had not said this to any individual angel. Marcus Dods sees this as referring to the resurrection and ascension. But the more likely reference is to the incarnation. Since the Son is eternal, it could not refer to a begetting in eternity (cf. John 1:1, 14). So it must mean the virgin birth of Jesus.

I will be to him a Father, and he shall be to me a son (v.5b). The second citation is 2 Samuel 7:14. The immediate reference there was to Solomon, but it was also regarded as messianic. However, the thought here as in the previous citation is that the Messiah was the Son of David. The point again is that at no time did God say this to an angel. Angels are God's servants, not his sons.

The third citation is not certain, but it probably refers to Psalm 97:7, "Worship him, all ye gods." The idea is that all subordinate powers are to worship the Messiah. The author included angels among such powers.

And again, when he bringeth in the first begotten into the world, he saith, And let all the angels of God worship him (v.6). Robertson points out that if **again** be taken with "bringeth in" it would refer to the second coming. But if it be regarded as in verse 5 it refers to the incarnation. This latter is more natural here. **First begotten** or "first-born" *(prōtokon)* does not mean that the Son is a created being. It is used in the sense of "Lord" of the universe as in Colossians 1:15. When Jesus was born in Bethlehem, he was worshipped by angels (Lk. 2:13 f.). So the Son is not equal with angels; he is their God.

And of the angels he saith, Who maketh his angels spirits, and his ministers a flame of fire (v.7). The fourth reference is to Psalm 104:4. This psalm praises the greatness and glory of God, "who maketh his angels spirits, and his ministers a flame of fire" (v.7). **Spirits** *(pneumata)* may also mean winds. **Ministers** *(leitourgous)* was used of priests ministering in the temple, or of anyone who rendered a public service.

The suggestion here could be that God causes his angels to serve even in the form of the elemental forces of wind and fire. But Westcott relates this verse to the phenomena which attended the giving of the law at Sinai. Wind and fire were evidence of the awesome power of God as expressed even through angels. However, the point of the author is that whereas angels are servants, the Son is the ruler.

But unto the Son he saith, Thy throne, O God, is for ever and ever: a sceptre of righteousness is the sceptre of thy kingdom. Thou hast loved righteousness and hated iniquity; therefore God, even thy God, hath anointed thee with the oil of gladness above thy fellows" (vv.8–9).

This fifth reference is to Psalm 45:6–7. Scholars are divided over whether **God** (O God) is vocative or nominative case. If vocative, it reads as in the King James Version. But if nominative, it would read, "Thy throne is God." Robertson says that either is possible from the grammar. Westcott holds to the latter, but others hold to the former.[4] The writer agrees with the former idea. The author had stressed the full deity of the Son. So here he called him "God." Whereas the angels change in their service (v.7), the Son has an eternal kingdom. He changes not.

His sceptre of rule is **righteousness.** This renders a word meaning rectitude, uprightness *(euthutētos).* His rule is characterized by this. Righteousness in verse 9 renders *dikaiosunē,* the righteousness which characterizes the nature of God. Because the Son loves this righteousness and hates lawlessness *(anomian),* rebellion against God, God the Father has anointed the Son with the oil of gladness. The verb rendered **anointed** is *chriō,* whence comes *Christos* or Christ. Israel's kings were anointed with oil symbolizing the presence of the Holy Spirit upon them. At his baptism the Son was anointed with the Holy Spirit.

As such he is **above thy fellows.** Above renders *para,* alongside, but the thought here is beside or beyond by comparison. **Fellow** renders *metochos.* It means partners or sharers (cf. Heb. 3:1, 14; 6:4; 12:8). Other than in this epistle it is found in the New Testament only in Luke 5:7. But it is found often in the papyri.[5] Here the angels are seen as partners with the Son in his work, but he rules over them.

The sixth citation is Psalm 102:25–27. **And, Thou Lord, in the beginning hast laid the foundation of the earth; and the heavens are the work of thine hands: they shall perish; but thou remainest; and they all shall wax old as doth a garment; and as a vesture shalt thou fold them up, and they shall be changed: but thou art the same, and thy years shall not fail** (vv.10–12). The comparison here is of the eternal Son as opposed to the temporal universe. This comparison is emphatic as seen by *su* (v.10) and *su de* (vv. 11–12).

In the first place, the Son created the universe, so he preceded it. It will eventually be destroyed, but he will remain. **Remainest** renders the strong compound word *diamenō,* abide through or beyond the destruction of the material universe. Using the figure of clothes, the author added that like an outer garment grows old; so will the universe. And yet the Son will abide to roll it up as a mantle and change it for a new one. (Cf. new heavens and earth, a redeemed natural universe in Rom. 8:19 ff.). But the Son is the same. He will not change, and his years shall not come to an end. He is eternal. He controls the destiny of the natural order; he is not controlled by it.

The seventh citation reaches a climax. It is taken from Psalm 110:1. **But to which of the angels said he at any time, Sit on my right hand, until I make thine enemies thy footstool?** (v.13).

This proves conclusively that the Son is superior to angels. He is destined to rule. This promise made through the psalmist is to be fulfilled in Messiah's kingdom. He will rule over a redeemed natural and spiritual universe. They will gladly own him as Lord. Even his enemies will be forced to bow before him and confess that he whom they rejected is Lord over all. But, alas, for them it will be everlastingly too late (cf. Phil. 2:10 f.). This promise is related to God's world-mission of redemption (cf. 10:12 f.).

5. The Ministry of Angels (1:14)

What then is the role of angels?

Are they not all ministering spirits, sent forth to minister for them who shall be heirs of salvation?

Ministering refers to both public service as of a citizen and also religious service. **Minister** renders *diakonian,* the most menial of service. Note the word "deacon" in it. They render this service to those who *are about to inherit salvation.* **Salvation** here does not refer to regeneration but to *glorification,* the full-salvation seen in the sum-total of rewards in heaven including the bodily resurrection. So they minister to the saints of God on earth.

This does not teach that each one has a guardian angel, but that angels are used for the good of God's people. By contrast, saints are to serve the Son; angels are to serve the saints. This was the author's final brush stroke as he portrayed the Son's superiority to angels—and, of course, the supreme revelation through Him.

Notes

1. *The Epistle to the Hebrews,* Macmillan, London, 1928, p. 3.
2. Robertson, *Word Pictures in the New Testament,* Broadman Press, Nashville, 1932, Vol. V., p. 335.
3. *Op. cit.,* pp. 13 f.
4. Archer, *op. cit.,* p. 20; Johannes Schneider, *The Letter to the Hebrews,* Eerdmans, Grand Rapids, 1957, p. 15.
5. See Moulton and Milligan, *The Vocabulary of the Greek New Testament,* Eerdmans, Grand Rapids, 1949, p. 406.

II. The Greater Responsibility

Since these Hebrew Christians were the beneficiaries of this supreme revelation, it naturally follows that they bore a greater responsibility to share it with a pagan world. It is to this responsibility that the author turned in chapter 2. In it he dealt with both the human and divine sides of God's redemptive world-mission.

1. The First Exhortation (2:1)

Therefore we ought to give the more earnest heed to the things which we have heard, lest at any time we should let them slip.

This is the first of five definite exhortations used by the author. How one sees the purpose of the epistle will determine his understanding of these. It should be noted, however, that no matter how expertly one may reason, if he begins with the wrong premise he will arrive at the wrong conclusion. As seen previously it is this writer's opinion that the purpose of Hebrews is to issue a call to a world-mission in proclaiming the Christian gospel. In a very real sense this first exhortation is a key verse as revealing the author's purpose. What is he saying in it?

Therefore renders two Greek words *dia touto,* because of this. Because of what? The author referred to his argument in chapter 1. Because of the superior Christian revelation these Hebrew Christians should act upon it. **Ought** translates *dei,* a third person singular verb expressing a moral and spiritual necessity. It is morally and spiritually necessary to give a more abundant heed to the things heard, or to this supreme revelation. They had heard and believed the gospel. But that was not enough. They should be more concerned as to developing in it and sharing it.

The key to this verse, and in large measure to the epistle, is the verb rendered "should let slip" (KJV). This Greek verb is *pararreō,* to drift or flow alongside or by. It carries the idea, as used by Xenophon (Cryop. IV. 52) of a river flowing alongside or by. Or it may mean a ship on the river being carried along past a given point.

The form of this verb used here is an aorist *passive* subjunctive, *pararuōmen.* The passive voice means that something is being done to the subject. It is a strange thing that so many interpreters translate it as an *active* voice, as if the subject were doing something to something else.

For instance, Robertson correctly gives the verb form as passive, but he translates it as though it were active, "we drift away." [1] Westcott comments, "The idea is not that of simple forgetfulness, but of being swept along past the sure anchorage which is within reach." [2] Schneider sees it as the readers severing themselves from the Word and thus severed from Christ. "With that act he enters the path that leads to eternal damnation." [3] Thomas sees it as a "boat being swept along past its anchorage." [4]

But note that the verb is first person plural, not first person singular. Even Manson sees the danger warned against as "that of 'drifting' in the sense of slipping away from, or losing hold upon, the Christian salvation." [5] However, he does qualify this by seeing "a letting slip of the reality of the Christian message."

These citations are sufficient to show the general trend of regarding the readers as doing something rather than having something done to them. The passive voice clearly demands the latter. They are being flowed by or drifted by.

It appears that the author saw his readers standing on the bank of a river seeing themselves being flowed by on the part of the river. The river corresponds to God's redemptive purpose for all men. It flows along through history regardless of how men may relate to it. Any given generation of God's people may choose to launch out into this stream filling their place in this world-mission. Or through neglect of God's call to stand idly on the bank and be flowed by as the river moves along. So it is not a case of the Christian losing his salvation. It is that of losing one's opportunity of being used of God in sharing this salvation with others.

Keep in mind the Exodus epic. Israel was redeemed from Egypt and entered into a covenant with Jehovah to be his priest-nation to the world (cf. Ex. 19:1–6). The covenant on God's part was conditioned by obedience on Israel's part. Note the "if" and "then" of Exodus 19:5. Through her failure to keep the "if" she lost her claim on the "then." The author of Hebrews warned his readers not to make the same mistake.

A given generation of God's people may through disobedience delay the accomplishment of God's redemptive purpose. But it will not defeat it completely. God's river flows along. Israel as a nation under the old covenant was flowed by. She lost her opportunity. The true Israel under the new covenant must not make the same mistake. This applies in the twentieth century as well as in the first.

2. The Peril of Failure (2:2–4)

In these verses the author argued from the lesser to the greater. What happened to Israel would happen in greater degree to the readers if they failed to honor their covenant to bear fruit in God's redemptive purpose (cf. John 15:16).

For if the word spoken by angels was stedfast, and every transgression and disobedience received a just recompense of reward (v.2).

The word spoken by angels reflects the idea that the revelation to Moses at Sinai was given through angels (cf. Acts 7:38, 53; Gal. 3:19). This is inclusive of the covenant relationship. **Stedfast** renders *bebaios.* This word was used in the papyri in the sense of a legally guaranteed security. Deissman holds that the verb *bebaioō* and its derivatives must always be read with the technical sense of a guarantee in mind (cf. Rom. 15:8).[6] This word was guaranteed by God as binding upon his chosen people.

Every singles out each **transgression** and act of **disobedience.** The former means "a stepping aside" or refusal to obey (cf. 3:12). The latter connotes "neglect to obey." So these include wilful rebellion and also neglect with respect to duty.

Each one of these on the part of Israel received **a just recompense** [giving back] **of reward.** The punishment fitted the crime. The idea is that under the old covenant it was less than under the new, but it was surely punished, nevertheless. The final and climaxing punishment was the nation's loss in not being used of God as his priest-nation (cf. Matt. 21:43). From this the author moved to the greater argument.

How shall we escape, if we neglect so great a salvation; which at first began to be spoken by the Lord, and was confirmed unto us by them that heard him? (v.3).

In the Greek text **we** is doubly emphatic. It is written out as well as being present in the verb form, and it comes at the front of the sentence. It refers to the readers and all other Christians as over against Israel under the old covenant. **Escape** renders a verb meaning to flee out of something, that something being "a just recompence of reward" greater than under the old covenant. The future middle form strongly relates it to the readers and all future Christian generations. The **neglect** is assumed as being true. They were actually neglecting this salvation.

But what did the author mean here by **salvation?** This word and its verb form are used in the New Testament in various ways. They may refer to being healed from disease (Mark 5:34), rescued from danger (Matt. 27:40; Phil. 1:19), justification or regeneration (Acts 16:31; Eph. 2:8), sanctification (Phil. 2:12), and glorification (Heb. 1:14; 9:28). In the sense of spiritual salvation the idea may be *regeneration, sanctification,* or *glorification.* The context must decide in each case.

One is saved or *justified* before God the second he receives Christ. That is a fixed relationship (Eph. 2:8, "saved" a perfect tense, a completed action). In that same second he is *sanctified,* or set apart to God's service. This is the basic meaning in the word sanctify (cf. John 17:19). In the Christian this is accomplished by the indwelling of the Holy Spirit (John 14:17; Eph. 1:13–14). Thus Christians are called "saints" or holy, sanctified ones (1 Cor. 1:2). "Saints" may not always act saintly, but they are saints nevertheless, dedicated to God's service. In that state they should develop and serve to the saving not of the soul but of the Christian life. To the degree that one does this he is saved or *glorified* in heaven, glorification including the bodily resurrection plus the sum-total of glory and reward in heaven. Thus it is correct to say, "I am saved" (justification), "I am being saved" (sanctification), "I will be saved" (glorification). The context decides the meaning in each usage.

In this light the writer sees **salvation** in Hebrews 2:3 as *sanctification* with the ultimate sense of *glorification.* The author was making a comparison between Israel redeemed out of Egyptian bondage (cf. 3:12; 6:4 ff.) and these Hebrew Christians who had been redeemed from the bondage of sin. The danger was not that of returning to either Egypt or an unredeemed state, but of failure to go forward in achieving the purpose of their being.

So salvation here corresponds to launching out into the river of God's world-mission of redemption. The readers were not repudiating their initial experience of regeneration. They were not about to lose a past experience but a future one. They were neglecting their sanctification or the purpose for which they had been redeemed, with the result that they were affecting their glorification. Theirs was a greater purpose; so to neglect it entailed a greater penalty. The penalty was a loss of opportunity and its attendant eternal reward and glory. To the carnal Christian this may not, at the moment, seem to be so great a penalty. But when seen in its eternal aspects it is terrible indeed.

This message of salvation in its fullest sense had been proclaimed by the Lord himself. Here the Son is referred to as **Lord,** which in the true Christian sense means Jehovah in flesh. This is in contrast to angels in verse 2. So the greater revelation, the greater penalty for failure. It was **confirmed** (*bebaioō,* v.2 "sted-fast") to **us,** including the author, by them that heard it firsthand from the Lord. Paul insisted that he had received the gospel and further revelations directly from the Lord (Gal. 1:11 f.).

God also bearing them witness, both in signs and wonders, and with divers miracles, and gifts of the Holy Ghost [Spirit], according to his own will (v.4).

This gospel had been guaranteed as true by a further witness from God himself. "Bearing witness" renders a triple-compound verb *sunepimartureō* [*sun* (with), *epi,* (upon or additional), *martureō,* (bear testimony as in a legal court or to testify to something such as witnessing for Christ)]. To the words of the Son and the apostles God had joined in giving witness or an additional guarantee to the truth proclaimed. This he did in accompanying **signs** (*sēmeiois,* used of Jesus' miracles as signs of his deity, John 2:11), **wonders** (wonderful works), and **many** [many-colored] powers" (works of power). For these in reverse order see Acts 2:22.

To these miracles were added **gifts** [note the plural] **of the Holy Ghost** [Spirit]. This does not refer to the *gift* of the Holy Spirit himself, but to the gifts which he bestowed on Christians to be used in God's service (1 Cor. 12:4 ff.). He bestowed these on different people "according to his own will." Each gift was designed to be used in God's world-mission. Each recipient should use them for this purpose. Failure to do this is to lose even the Spirit-bestowed gift (cf. Matt. 25:28 f.). To say nothing of the reward for its intended purpose.

3. The Human Responsibility (2:5-8)

God has not given this world-mission responsibility to angels but unto redeemed human beings. Jesus' various commissions to evangelize the world were given to those who had received him as Savior. God covenants for spiritual service only with redeemed people (cf. Ex. 19:1-6; Matt. 28:18 ff.). So in these verses the author showed that God has given men the task of subduing the universe natural and spiritual.

For unto the angels hath he not put in subjection the world to come, whereof we speak (v.5). The Greek text begins with the negative particle *ou,* so it is an emphatic negative statement. The new order **whereof we speak,** the spiritual restoration of the world both natural and spiritual, is not to be subdued by angels. The verb rendered **put in subjection** is one meaning to line up in order troops under command. In a sense it means to bring order out of chaos. **World** translates *oikoumenēn* (note, "ecumenical") which means those who dwell in the same house. In the sense here it speaks of "the inhabited earth," though the context **to come** points to the future, namely, a redeemed and subdued order, the messianic age or kingdom. Angels were not given responsibility for creating the conditions for such. It is the responsibility of redeemed human beings working through the Holy Spirit under the lordship of Jesus Christ.

Of interest in this regard is the account in Matthew 28. In the resurrection of Jesus the redemptive work of God in Christ was finished. God sent an angel to open the tomb, something the women could not do, and to tell them of the resurrection. Then the angel told them to relay word to the disciples to meet Jesus, the living Lord, in Galilee. Having done so, the angel said, "Lo, I have told you" (v.7). These were his last words to them. He had done all that an angel could do. From then on God placed the responsibility of declaring the message of redemption upon the people of Christ (vv. 18-20). So in God's providence the future success of his redemptive world-mission rests in the hands of his people.

To substantiate his statement in verse 5, the author cited God's commission that man should have dominion over the natural order (cf. Gen. 2:28). Note the three areas of dominion: sea, sky or space, and earth. Man is to explore and subdue all these for his good and God's glory.

What is man, that thou art mindful of him? or the son of man, that thou visitest him? (v.6). This through verse 8*a* is a quotation from Psalm 8:4-6. It has reference to man or mankind, not to Jesus. It was never considered as messianic but as designed to show the dignity and glory of man which can be realized fully only in the Christ. **The son of man** in the Greek text reads "son of man." When this phrase is used of Jesus it reads "the Son of the man."

From man's viewpoint this verse expresses the seeming insignificance of man as compared to the rest of God's creation (cf. Psalm 8:3). Why should God hold him in mind or *visit* him as in the Garden of Eden? Or in the person of his Son for redemption? Men may hold other men in contempt, but God never does. No man made in God's image should be despised by another man. For every man is of infinite dignity and worth in God's sight. Of course, man through his sin was separated from God. And that is the very reason for God's redemptive world-mission. Man's true dignity and destiny can be realized only in Christ.

Having expressed the lowly state of man (v.6), the author expressed three things about man as to his nature, honor, and destiny (vv. 7–8).**Thou madest him a little lower than the angels; thou crownedest him with glory and honour, and didst set him over the works of thy hands"** (v.7; cf. v.9).

The author quoted Psalm 8 from the Septuagint and so used the word "angels." But the Hebrew word in Psalm 8 is *Elohim,* the general word for "God." Westcott says that this usage should mean not God but "a little less than one who has a divine nature." [7] Robertson cites the use of *Elohim* for judges in Psalm 82:1. Then he comments, "Here it is certainly not 'God' in our sense." [8] Delitzsch recognizes the true sense of *Elohim* but justifies the reading in the Septuagint as "angels." [9]

However, this writer sees no major problem at this point. The Hebrew had several names for God, *Elohim* being one of them. This word was used of false gods also. When the Hebrew people referred to the one true God, they used *Yahweh* or Jehovah (cf. Ex. 6:3; Deut. 6:4 f.). The Greek had but one name for God, *Theos.* So when the translators of the Septuagint came to Psalm 8:5 their strong monotheism led them to substitute "angels" for *Elohim.*

But the reading in the Hebrew text is true of man as God created him, in God's image and likeness (Gen. 1:27). He was created as a person endowed with the right of choice. It was in the wrong use of choice that man fell from this image and likeness. It is God's purpose in redemption to restore man to his original estate. Thus those who receive his Son in faith shall become sons of God (John 1:12; Rom. 8:16 f.).

So man was created a little lower than God, not angels. Nowhere does the Bible place angels above man in dignity and honor (cf. 1:14). Man's original sin was when he tried to be God. For "gods" in Genesis 3:5 translates *Elohim,* the same word used in Genesis 1:1. Man was made a little lower than God. It was when through inordinate ambition he tried to be God or to be equal with him that man lost his spiritual relation to God. But the fact remains that he was created a little lower than God.

The second thing the author says about man is that God **crownedest him with glory and honour** (v.7*b*). **And didst set him over the works of thy hands** is not in the best manuscripts, but it is found in essence in verse 8.

This glory and honour refers to man's dignity as a person. In this sense he is akin to God's nature. Of no other of God's creatures is it said that it "became a living soul" (Gen. 2:7). Other creatures have animal life or "breath." And are akin to the "dust" since their bodies are composed of the elements. Man likewise is akin to the elements, "formed . . . of the dust of the ground," and to animal life, "breathed into his nostrils the breath of life" (Gen. 2:7). But only man is akin to God in spirit. He is mortal, his natural life will end (Gen. 2:17). He is natural, and at death his body will return to dust (Gen. 3:19). But his spirit is immortal. Either he will *exist* eternally without God, or else he will *live* eternally in God. It is for this reason that God's world-mission of redemption is so vitally important.

Thou hast put all things in subjection under his feet. For in that he put all in subjection under him, he left nothing that is not put under him. But now we see not yet all things put under him (v.8).

This is the third comment that the author made about man. This, of course, refers back to Genesis 1:26–28 (cf. 2:15, 19–20). Man in God's plan was to have dominion over sea, sky, and earth, including every other creature on earth. He was to be fruitful, multiply, and replenish the earth, and to subdue it. Our verse says that God has **put all things** in subjection under man's feet. This is the verb for lining up troops under command. And **all things** renders *panta* without the definite article, or every single part of the universe.

However, when man through sin lost his spiritual relation to God, he lost his spiritual relation to nature as well. For in a sense unknown to man nature itself *fell* and even now longs for its redemption. Strangely its redemption is related to man's redemption even as its fall was related to man's fall (cf. Rom. 8:19–23).

Following man's fall nature became his enemy, not his ally (Gen. 3:17–19). Both nature and man on the prowl are the works of Satan (Job 1:12–19). The same is true of disease (Job. 2:5 ff.). However, God's original purpose stands. Man is to have dominion, even though his sin has made it more difficult.

From *panta* in verse 8*a* the author changed to *ta panta* in verse 8*b*. The universe as a whole, natural and spiritual, God has put in subjection under man. **Nothing** *(oude)*, not even one thing is excepted. And then the awesome note: **But now we see not yet all things** [*ta panta*] **put under him.**

Despite difficulties man has done a pretty good job in subduing the natural universe. He has even gone to the moon, and now looks longingly at the stars. With the multiplication of knowledge and inventions, who can say what man can or cannot do?

However, in subduing the spiritual universe man has not done so well. With war, crime, violence, hatred, and man's other inhumanity to man raging throughout the earth men despair. *Outer space* has yielded in measure to man. But *inner space* is still a vast wilderness. Paganism holds the vast majority of men in its clutches.

Is not this because God's people have been so indifferent to God's world-mission? If they had worked as hard and long at evangelizing the hearts of men as they have in securing creature comforts, the wilderness would be glad and spiritual deserts would long since have blossomed as a rose.

4. The Role of Jesus (2:9–10)

From a note of defeatism the author turned to one of eager anticipation. Man in his own strength and lack of endeavor has failed, but there is still hope.

But we see Jesus, who was made a little lower than the angels for the suffering

of death, crowned with glory and honour; that he by the grace of God should taste death for every man (v.9).

In the Greek text the opening and emphatic words are "But the one made a little lower than the angels." Then follows "We see Jesus through the suffering of death." The point is that in order to give victory in subduing the natural and spiritual universe God in the Son has taken on man's nature, apart from sin (cf. 4:15). Here **little** may read "a little while," referring not only to the degree but duration of this identity with man. The same words applied to men in verse 7*a* the author here applied to Jesus.

This is the first time that the author used the name "Jesus." He who eternally bears the nature of *Son* became flesh as *Jesus,* Jehovah is salvation. The reference, of course, is to the incarnation whereby God moved in history to provide for and to set forward historically his eternal purpose of redemption.

But how do we see Jesus? Not simply as a good man, noble example, or excellent teacher. "We see Jesus through the suffering of death, crowned with glory and honour, that he by the grace of God should taste death for every man." Thus by God's grace Jesus, the complete Man, is able to restore each single man to the place of glory and honor in which God created him. For any man to be complete he must be *in Christ.* And this through his faith in the atoning work of Jesus.

For it became him, for whom are all things, and by whom are all things, in bringing many sons to glory, to make the captain of their salvation perfect through sufferings (v.10).

Became means to be becoming or seemly. **Him** refers to God, not to Christ. **For whom . . . by whom** expresses purpose and means respectively. The universe as a whole (*ta panta,* repeated after each of the above) came into being for God and by his creative power. Yet he who is thus related to the universe was so concerned to bring **many sons to glory,** that he was in Christ reconciling man unto himself (2 Cor. 5:19). This answers the question asked in verse 6, "What is man?" If God is so concerned about saving men, can his people be less concerned?

Captain renders a word *(archēgon)* which means one going before to lead as a prince or other leader. It may also be translated "author." So Jesus Christ is the Author of salvation in its full sense of justification, sanctification, and glorification. By God's grace he provided for it. But he is also the Leader or Captain leading his forces to storm with the gospel the citadels of men's sinful hearts.

He was made **perfect** through sufferings. Perfect here does not mean to become free from flaw. For Jesus had none. The Greek word is an aorist infinitive *(teleiōsai)* of *teleioō,* to bring something to its intended end, to fulfil its purpose. So Jesus was brought to his intended end; he fulfilled his purpose as Redeemer, through sufferings.

If this be true of him, it naturally follows that his people should fulfil their reason for being by doing the same in filling their place in God's world-mission of redemption. If they neglect the fellowship of suffering, they shall also miss the glory, and no suffering can compare with that glory (Rom. 8:17 f.).

5. The Fellowship of Service (2:11-18)

As Christ identified himself with men for their redemption, so is he identified with the redeemed in service. As he gave himself to accomplish God's redemptive purpose, so must they do the same in the world-mission to share that redemption with a lost world.

For both he that sanctifieth and they that are sanctified are all one: for which cause he is not ashamed to call them brethren (v.11) Jesus is the one who sanctifies believers (9:13 f.; 13:12). The words for *sanctify* are singular and plural participles respectively. The former is active voice and the latter is passive voice. So Jesus is "the one sanctifying" and believers are the ones being sanctified.

The root verb is *hagiazō*, to sanctify or make holy. The word *hagios* means saint or holy one. It was applied to all Christians (cf. 2 Cor. 1:1). Of interest is the fact that in the Old Testament the word holy applies primarily to things; in the New Testament it is used mostly of people.

The root meaning of the verb is to set apart or dedicate to the service of a god or God. In religions based upon sex *holy*—set apart—men and women were used in their temples in worship through the sex act. It is evident, therefore, that originally the word carried no moral content. This came to be applied to it as it was related to the true God. But still the basic idea was separation or dedication. While basically the words *sanctify* and *sanctification* do not connote being rid of sin, it is clear that one set apart to God's service should be a clean vessel.

Jesus sanctified himself to God's redemptive purpose (cf. John 17:19). but he also sanctifies his people that they may become instruments in furthering that purpose. "All of one" reads "out of one all" *(ex henos pantes)*. This anticipates the word **brethren.** Jesus is not ashamed to call the sanctified ones by this name. He is God's Son essentially and eternally. Believers become sons of God (cf. John 1:12). But they have a mutual relation to the Father. Paul shows that while this sonship shared with Jesus carries privileges, it also entails responsibilities (Rom. 8:17 f.). So the sanctified ones share with Jesus the obligation to suffer in carrying forward God's redemptive mission.

Now the question arises as to whether sanctification is an instantaneous experience, or is it a process by which the believer becomes progressively free from sin and dedicated to God? Since the participles in verse 11 are present tenses, many see this as a process, that Christ keeps on santifying believers. This, of course, is grammatically correct. But the present tense may also read that an action is done from time to time or repeatedly as the occasion demands. For instance, Acts 2:47 reads, "And the Lord added to the church daily such as should be saved." "Such as should be saved" translates a present passive participle, the same as *hagiazomenoi* in verse 11. Acts 2:47 does not mean the ones predestined to salvation, or that they were saved over and over, or that they were saved by a process. It properly should read, "the ones from time to time being saved." As each one was saved he was added to the church.

So in Hebrews 2:11 Jesus is the one sanctifying from time to time those who from time to time were being saved. While Jesus sanctifies he does so through the Holy Spirit. Believers become sons of God through the Holy Spirit on the basis of Jesus' redeeming work (cf. Rom. 8:9–16). And Jesus sanctifies them through the indwelling Spirit. Regeneration is an instantaneous experience wrought by the Holy Spirit (John 3:3–8). At the same moment the Spirit indwells the believer as God's guarantee that he is saved and will be kept saved (Eph. 1:13–14; cf. John 14:17). It is then that the believer is sanctified or set apart to God's service. Though he may be *unsaintly* by moral standards, he is a *saint*, a holy, set apart, dedicated one (2 Cor. 1:1). True, he must grow and develop in that state of sanctification. In such he must become involved in the service of God. And Christ through the Holy Spirit enables the *saint* to do just that.

This is what Hebrews is all about. The readers were on "dead center," and the author sought to send them on their way in both developing and serving in their state of sanctification. They were to emulate the example of their Saviour, who sanctified himself to do God's redemptive will. He has also sanctified them, and they should be about the business of God.

The author supported the statement about Christ's oneness with his brethren by citing three Old Testament verses (vv. 12–13). **I will declare thy name unto my brethren, in the midst of the church will I sing praise unto thee** (v.12; cf. Psalm 22:22). It is significant that Psalm 22 is a messianic psalm which remarkably describes Jesus' crucifixion. It is for this reason, his death and resurrection, that Jesus can call believers **brethren.** The scene here is one of a congregation assembled for worship with Jesus in the midst (cf. Matt. 18:20).

The other citations are from Isaiah 8:17–18. **I will put my trust in him. . . . Behold I and the children which God hath given me** (v.13). Jesus trusted in the Father, and his " brethren" must do the same thing as they fill their place in the redemptive mission. They are **children** through faith in Jesus; through their faithfulness other "children" will be added unto him.

The fellowship between Jesus and his brethren is further emphasized as the author showed His identity with them in his redemptive act and continuing help in their Christian lives. These things add all the more to their obligation in the world-mission.

Forasmuch then as the children are partakers of flesh and blood, he also himself likewise took part of the same; that through death he might destroy him that had the power of death, that is, the devil (v.14).

Are partakers renders the perfect passive form of *koinōneō,* to share or have things in common. A derivative of this verb, *koinōnia,* is used for fellowship among believers. The verb form means that all men, including the **children,** have a common bond in their **blood and flesh.** So Christ became the same, apart from sin, that he might die for man's sin. **Took part** renders *metechō* (see 3:1, *metochoi,* noun form). It is practically synonymous with *koinōneō,* its primary thought being that of *partners.* Christ became partners with men, except for sin, that he might save them from sin.

Men are flesh and blood; he became flesh and blood (cf. John 1:14). Men are sinners; he became sin for them that through him they might receive the righteousness of God (cf. 2 Cor. 5:21). His incarnation was for the purpose of destroying the devil and his work (cf. 1 John 3:8).

Actually the word rendered **might destroy** is *katargeō*. This verb means to render inoperative. The picture is that of a machine which receives its power by way of a pulley belt. When the pulley belt is disengaged, the power is shut off rendering the machine inoperative. So in his death and resurrection Christ removed the source of the devil's power. He rendered him inoperative as He conquered spiritual death and in its place gave life. Ultimately, even physical death will be rendered inoperative through Christ in the resurrection from the dead (cf. 1 Cor. 15:25 f.).

And deliver them who through fear of death were all their lifetime subject to bondage (v.15).

Deliver means to change from or to free from bondage. Throughout their lifetime men are slaves to the fear of death, but Christ has removed death's sting (cf. 1 Cor. 15:45–57). And though men still have the will to live, they need not fear death for beyond lies the assurance of life everlasting to all who believe in Jesus.

Of interest is Paul's word following his assurance of victory over death. "Therefore, my beloved brethren, be ye stedfast, unmoveable, always abounding in the work of the Lord, forasmuch as ye know that your labour is not in vain in the Lord" (1 Cor. 15:58). And while the author of Hebrews did not say so specifically, this is the import of his words in 2:14–15. In the assurance of their victory over sin and death through Christ, they are to share it with others through their God-given world-mission.

For verily he took not on him the nature of angels; but he took on him the seed of Abraham (v.16). He did this to accomplish this victory. Had he come as an angel Christ would have been entirely different from men. But as **the seed of Abraham** he was one with them apart from sin.

It was through Abraham and his seed that all the families of the earth should be blessed (cf. Gen. 12:1–3). This was God's covenant of redemption, a covenant of grace. Paul identified this "seed" with Christ (Gal. 3:16). He further said that those who believe in him are "Abraham's seed, and heirs according to the promise" (Gal. 3:29). In Romans 8:17 f. he spoke of heirship as entailing both privilege and responsibility. So the readers of Hebrews are Abraham's seed through Christ. And along with the *blessing* they are *to be a blessing* (Gen. 12:2).

Thus they are to commit themselves to God's world-mission which he began historically in his covenant of grace with Abraham. As God's people they are also under a covenant of service as seen in the Mosaic covenant to which the author moves in chapter 3.

Wherefore in all things it behoved him to be made like unto his brethren, that he might be a merciful and faithful high priest in things pertaining to God, to make reconciliation for the sins of the people (v.17).

Christ's identity with his **brethren** is to accomplish reconciliation. The verb rendered **made like** *(homoioō)* calls for attention. It means that while Christ resembled man as flesh and blood, he was also different from man in that he was also God. Commenting on Paul's use of this word, Arndt and Gingrich [6] in Romans 8:3, "likeness of sinful flesh," and Philippians 2:7, "likeness of men," note two possible meanings. It could mean that Christ in the flesh

> possessed a completely human form and that his physical body was capable of sinning as human bodies are, or that he had only the form of a man and was looked upon as a human being . . . whereas in reality he remained a Divine Being even in this world. In the light of what Paul says about Jesus in general it is safe to assert that his use of our word is to bring out both that Jesus in his earthly career was similar to sinful men and yet not absolutely like them.

With this the writer agrees, provided that "similar to sinful men" means that in his flesh Jesus was *capable* of sinning, yet did not sin. Otherwise, the incarnation was not complete. He was God. But he was also Man. He was not God simply pretending to be a man. For further discussion on this see 4:15.

Jesus' identity with man was to the end that he might be a High Priest sympathetic to man in his sin and faithful to God in providing cleansing from sin (cf. 1:3; 2:9; 3:1). He ministered before God to make propitiation for man's sin. This refers to the function of the high priest on the Day of Atonement. Annually he made sacrifices in the Holy Place and carried the blood into the Holy of Holies to atone for sin for that year. Christ did this in his once-for-all sacrifice making not an annual but a full atonement for man's sin. The act of the high priest made the people temporarily clean that they might serve God. In his act Jesus did the same that believers might be perpetually fitted for his service.

For in that he himself hath suffered being tempted, he is able to succour them that are tempted (v.18).

Not only did Jesus atone for man's sin, he is qualified by experience to aid believers in their struggle against temptation (see 4:15 for full discussion). Jesus himself knew the fires of temptation. Therefore, he is a "merciful" or sympathetic High Priest. The temptations of Jesus recorded in the Gospels were related to his mission of redemption. Satan repeatedly sought to divert him from God's will in this regard (cf. Matt. 4:1–11; 16:21–23; John 6:14 f.). Jesus knew the agony of soul involved in such testing.

These temptations are significant with respect to the purpose of Hebrews. The readers then were being tempted to turn aside from their place in God's redemptive world-mission. So out of his own experience in this regard Christ **is able to succour them that are tempted** in the same manner. **Succour** renders the verb *boētheō*, to run in response to a cry for help. Note this same verb in Matthew 15:25, "Lord, help me."

There is no reason, then, for the Christian's failure to persevere in God's world-mission. He follows One who faced the same problem and won the victory.

And through faith in him all who are tempted to falter may find him running to aid them when they cry, "Lord, help me." It is for this reason, plus the message they have to deliver, that Christians bear the greater responsibility over those under the partial revelation of God.

Notes

1. *Op. cit.,* p. 342; cf. Archer, *op. cit.,* p. 22; Neil, *The Epistle to the Hebrews,* SCM Press, London, 1959, p. 37.
2. *Op. cit.,* p. 37.
3. *Op. cit.,* pp. 18 f.
4. *Op. cit.,* p. 30; cf. Wuest, *Hebrews in the Greek New Testament,* Eerdmans, Grand Rapids, 1953. p. 51.
5. *Op. cit.,* p. 48.
6. See Hobbs, *Preaching Values from the Papyri,* Baker, Grand Rapids, 1964, pp. 33 f.
7. *Op. cit.,* p. 44.
8. *Op. cit.,* p. 345.
9. *Commentary on Hebrews,* Vol. 1., Eerdmans, Grand Rapids, 1952, pp. 103 ff.
6. *A Greek-English Lexicon of the New Testament,* University Press, Cambridge, 1952, p. 570.

III. The Lack of Faith

Up to this time the author has made three major points. He has shown that his readers are the beneficiaries of God's supreme revelation in Jesus Christ. Also he has shown that Christ has revealed God as redeeming love, whereby he has provided redemption for all who will believe in his Son for salvation. Interwoven in these two points is the third, namely, his readers' greater responsibility to share this revelation and redemption with others by filling their place in God's world-mission of redemption. He warned them not to lose their opportunity by being flowed by on the part of this redemptive purpose.

Beginning in chapter 3 the author enlarged upon the various thoughts expressed somewhat in embryo. It will be seen that he plunged completely into the Exodus epic from which he drew other warnings against failure to fit into the world-mission.

In chapter 3 he used Moses as his example, moving toward Israel's rebellion against her covenant of service as a priest-nation. And he pointed out the consequence of that rebellion, applying it to his readers.

1. The Comparison with Moses (3:1–2)

As Moses was God's servant in making His covenant with the nation Israel, so Christ is the one who activated the new covenant with the true Israel, the Christian people. So the author began by comparing the two.

Wherefore, holy brethren, partakers of the heavenly calling, consider the Apostle and High Priest of our profession, Christ Jesus (v. 1).

As therefore (*dia touto,* 2:1) pointed back to the supreme revelation, **wherefore** *(othen)* points back to both that and the greater responsibility. Commenting on *othen* Westcott says, "Wherefore, because Christ has taken our nature to Himself, and knows our needs and is able to satisfy them." [1] This is true, but as seen above it appears to encompass all that has preceded it in the epistle.

Note that the author addresses his readers as **holy brethren.** This shows that they are Hebrew Christians, not Jews contemplating becoming such. In the Greek text the words are reversed "brethren holy." They are brethren in Christ and sanctified or set apart for God's service by Christ (cf. 2:11).

Furthermore, he called them **partakers of the heavenly calling.** What did he mean by "partakers"? Unfortunately, the English word has come to mean largely to share in something received, such as partaking of a meal. But what is the meaning of the Greek word which it translates here?

The word is *metochoi* (see 2:14), the plural of *metochos*. The verb form is *metechō*. It is composed of *meta*, with, among, or being in the company of another; and *echo*, to have or hold. So *metechō* means to have or hold with another as in partnership or joint participation. As noted under 2:14 it is practically synonymous with *koinōneō*, to have in common or to share in something.

These verbs are used jointly in the papyri. For instance, one example reads, "there are many methods of giving them (viz. robbers) shelter: some do so because they are partners [*koinōnountes*] in their misdeeds, others without sharing [*metechontes*] in these yet." The word "sharing" might just as well read "partners." An example of *metechō* alone reads, "as I am unable *to take part* in the cultivation" (author's italics). Or as a partner in a joint enterprise.

The word *metochos* is also found repeatedly in the papyri in the sense of partners. One example will suffice: "Through Pasitos and the partners." [2] Of note is the fact that this word is translated as "partners" in Luke 5:7.

The author of Hebrews has a fondness for both *metechō* and *metochos*. The former is found here three out of eight times used in the New Testament. The latter is used five times, found elsewhere in the New Testament only in Luke 5:7. Strange to say the meaning of "partners" in the papyri is found in the King James Version only in Luke where the context demands it. Peter, Andrew, James, and John were partners in the fishing business. But in Hebrews (1:9; 3:1,14; 6:4; 12:8) it is always rendered as "partakers." With the possible exception of 12:8 "partners" seems to be the better reading.

Metochos is one of the key words in Hebrews. It is for this reason that this analysis is merited. If the reading be "partakers" the sense is that of *receiving* something from God, e.g., salvation. If it be "partners" the sense is that of *sharing* in a common responsibility. As this study proceeds the writer believes that "partners" will prove to be the better reading. Indeed, one wonders if "partakers" is not the result of the translators' belief that one can have salvation and then lose it. Perhaps a more charitable position is that they did not have the benefit of the papyri. However, there still remains the problem between Luke 5:7 and the passages in Hebrews. But in the light of the papyri it weighs the evidence in favor of "partners."

So the author addresses his readers as "partners in the heavenly calling." Literally, "of a heavenly calling." Robertson sees this as a call "from heaven and is to heaven in its appeal." [3] Manson has something of the same idea. He sees it as a call to salvation but with emphasis on the eschatological aspects of the Christian life or its final consummation in heaven. Perhaps so, if one keeps in mind the threefold nature of salvation as justification, sanctification, and glorification. But the author's primary emphasis seems to be on sanctification.

Keep in mind the Exodus epic. Israel was called *out* of Egyptian bondage; then, she was called *to* a world-mission. How she filled that place determined her degree of glorification or her pleasing God and receiving his reward. As seen in **holy brethren** the author is writing to a redeemed people. The trend of his argument seems to point primarily to the here-and-now rather than to an eschatological hope. It is secondary to the author's purpose.

Like Israel these Hebrew Christians are called to a world-mission. As such they are *partners* in their calling, partners with Jesus (3:1,14) and with the Holy Spirit (6:4). The immediate thought is their partnership with Jesus, who has provided the redemption which they are to propagate through the power of the Holy Spirit.

So he called them to **consider** or "put their minds down on" *(katanoeō)* Jesus. Since the verb is an imperative he commanded them to do so, showing the urgency of the matter. Since they have this calling they should put their minds on "the Apostle and High Priest of our profession, Jesus." "Christ" is not in the best manuscripts.

Already the author had anticipated the High Priest idea (cf. 2:17) and returned to it later. But he introduced a new title "Apostle." It means one sent forth. In this case sent forth on a mission for God, a redemptive mission (cf. 2:9–18). The author will also deal with this idea later (cf. 10:5 ff.).

For the moment it is sufficient to note two things. One, in the New Testament the term "apostle" was used not only of the Twelve but of pioneers in the work of spreading the gospel (cf. Eph. 4:11 f.). They were followed by others who served in districts or local churches. The office of apostle corresponds to missionary. These are Greek and Latin words with the same idea.

Jesus was God's Apostle sent into the world as his *Pioneer* in providing redemption (cf. 12:2, "author"). To the Twelve Jesus said, "As my Father hath sent me [*apestalken*, perfect of *apostellō*, a complete, final sending forth], also I am sending [present tense of *pempō*] you" (John 20:21). Often Jesus spoke of the Father sending him, using both verbs. Here he used them both in practically the same sense.

Many years ago in a seminary chapel service Dr. W. O. Carver introduced Dr. Everett Gill, Sr. as a "foreign missionary." Dr. Gill responded, "No, I am not a *foreign* missionary. The world has had but one foreign missionary, Jesus, who was sent by the Father to the earth. I am just a *missionary* serving in Europe as you young preachers serve in areas near this campus."

Yes, Jesus was God's *Apostle* sent from heaven to earth. All Christians should be Jesus' *apostles* sent throughout the earth.

Profession or confession, one's avowal of Jesus as Lord and Saviour also appears in 4:14; 10:23. One should own Jesus not only as Saviour but as Lord. If one obeys the lordship of Jesus, he will go as he has been sent (cf. Matt. 28:18 ff.; Luke 24:47–49; John 20:21 ff.; Acts 1:8). The fact that the author used "Jesus" without "Christ" (best texts) is suggestive. It seems to focus the thought on his earthly mission apart from the cosmic or eschatological aspects. Jesus had finished his mission of redemption. The readers should be busy about declaring it to a lost world. This is suggested in verses 2 ff.

Who was faithful to him that appointed him, as also Moses was faithful in

all his house (v.2).

This verse introduces the comparison and contrast between Jesus and Moses. Both were related to covenants made with God's people. And in the allegorical sense Moses was Jehovah's "apostle" sent into Egypt to be the human means of redeeming Israel from bondage. He figured in the Exodus epic as Jesus did in the *Christian epic*. Likewise, Moses had predicted the coming of a Prophet "like unto me; unto him ye shall hearken" (Deut. 18:15). This within itself suggests the greater obligation of these Hebrew Christians to hear and obey Jesus.

Jesus was faithful in his mission even as Moses was in his. **In all his house** refers back to Numbers 12:7. The occasion was rebellion against Moses' leadership on the part of his sister and brother, Miriam and Aaron (Deut. 12:1 f.). In authenticating Moses' leadership, Jehovah said that any other prophet he would speak to in a dream or vision. It would not be so to Moses, for Jehovah would speak to him "mouth to mouth" (v.8). For Moses "is faithful in all mine house" (v.7). Note "mine house." So **his house** in Hebrews 3:2 is God's house or the office which Moses held in God's purpose.

This suggests that the Hebrew Christians as Jesus' "brethren" were rebelling against his leadership. Moses was trying to lead Israel into Canaan, the land of her destiny (cf. chapter 4), and his brethren were in rebellion. "Hath the Lord indeed spoken only by Moses? hath he not spoken also by us?" (Num. 12:2). Jesus was seeking to lead his "brethren" into the fulfilment of their world-mission. But, in effect, they were despising his missionary commissions, saying that their uncommitted wills were as binding as his. Israel's failure to enter Canaan was not Moses' fault, for he was faithful to his charge. The failure was the rebellion of Israel (cf. vv. 7 ff.). So failure in the world-mission is not due to Jesus who faithfully discharged his mission. The failure is that of his rebellious people.

2. The Contrast to Moses (3:3–6)

From this comparison the author moved to a contrast between Jesus and Moses. As faithful as was Moses, he did not compare in greatness to Jesus. For that reason rebellion against Jesus' will is more serious than that against the will of Moses.

For this man was counted worthy of more glory than Moses, inasmuch as he who hath builded the house hath more honour than the house. For every house is builded by some man; but he that built all things is God (vv.3–4).

The figure here is that the builder is superior to the house that he builds. **Inasmuch as** may read "so much as." The contrast is proportionate as a house is to a builder. The house is the product of the man. So to that degree the man is the greater. Who can compare a person with a structure?

So Jesus is the builder. And Moses is only a part of the spiritual house that He is building. Thus in infinite degree Jesus' glory is the greater. **Counted worthy** renders a verb which has in it the idea of weights. Put Moses' glory on one side of the scales and Jesus' glory on the other side. The latter infinitely outweighs the former.

And Moses verily was faithful in all his house, as a servant, for a testimony of those things which were to be spoken of after (v.5).

Moses was a servant in God's house. His role was but to give witness to that which would be declared openly at a future time. He witnessed dimly of God's redemptive purpose. Christ revealed it fully. Note that in verse 6 "Christ" is used rather than "Jesus." Christ is eternally the one bearing the relation to God of Son (cf. 1:2) in his own house.

Whose house are we, if we hold fast the confidence and the rejoicing of the hope firm unto the end (v.6; cf. v.14).

What does the author mean by these words? In the English reading one could clearly see the idea that one is saved only if he endures until the end of life. Which, of course, allows for apostasy in the common usage of the word. But if this be the meaning, it conflicts with other New Testament teachings to the contrary. The Bible does not contradict itself. This alone should give caution as to meaning.

When there is a seeming contradiction in the English, one should resort to the Greek text. Interpreters speak of the "original Greek." What is the *original* Greek in terms of the Koine Greek of the New Testament? Unfortunately, the Greek words have through the years picked up theological debris. Happily there is a source by which to test Koine meanings. It is the papyri: the letters, bills, and other documents used in the ordinary affairs of life in the period contemporary to the New Testament.

Before the recent discovery of the papyri, it was thought that the Greek of the New Testament, different from Classical Greek, was a special language found originally only in the New Testament. One German scholar, R. Rothe, even called it "a language of the Holy Ghost." The discovery of the papyri changed this. Doctor Adolf Deissmann discovered that the Greek of the papyri was the same as that in the New Testament. Rather than a language of the Holy Spirit, it was the common or Koine language of everyday communication. A flood of papyri has been discovered. Thus, today less than fifty words in the New Testament have not been found in the papyri or other current writings.

So to get back to the *original* Greek in the New Testament one should examine its words as used in the papyri. In that light what did the author's first readers understand him to say? For that is what he says to present-day readers.

Certain key words call for examination: **firm unto the end,** and **hold fast.** The first phrase is bracketed by both Nestle and Westcott. This means that its genuineness here is questioned. One major manuscript (B) does not have it. But it is without question genuine in verse 14. It certainly fits both verses, so is treated here.

In order to see it clearly it should be read in the Greek. *Mechri telous bebaion. Telous* is a form of the word *telos* meaning distance, goal, or end. Hence, telephone, telegraph, television; voice, writing, or vision projected to a desired goal or end. In the papyri *bebaion* is used in the sense of a guarantee. It was used in commercial and legal documents in this way. A good example is the following: "And I will further guarantee [*bebaios*] the property always against all claims with every guarantee [*bebaiōsis*]." Another use is in a guarantee that there is no debt against property by the fiscal authorities. Both the verb and noun forms are found frequently in this sense.⁴ And this meaning throws light upon their uses in the New Testament (cf. Rom. 4:16; 15:8; 1 Cor. 1:6; 2 Cor. 1:7; Heb. 2:2 f.).

Hold fast renders the verb *katechō,* combining *echo,* to have, with the preposition *kata,* which intensifies the verb. It might be rendered "really to have." This verb is used often in the papyri in the sense of possessing something.⁵ For instance, it is used for possessing territory. One example reads, "Shall have the legal ownership of the lands which they have possessed." Another usage reads, "When I wished to know on what pretext it came about that Egyptian wives have by native Egyptian law a claim upon their husband's property through their marriage contracts." One case speaks of a person having become owner of a house. Cf. 1 Corinthians 7:30 and 2 Corinthians 6:10. So one may see the idea of possession in Hebrews 3:6,14.

Look at other words in this verse. **Confidence** renders *parresian* which carries the idea of boldness which is expressed in word or deed. **Rejoicing** *(kauchēma)* may be translated as glory or boasting, the former probably applying here.

Now in the light of these things this verse may be read: "Whose house are we, if the boldness and the glory of the hope until the end guaranteed we possess." It does not mean that one is a part of the family of Christ only if he holds on to his hope until the end of life. But that he is in that family if he really possesses such a hope. And this he has if he has believed in Christ. Once he does, he has a hope or assurance which is guaranteed to abide throughout this life and beyond. The idea of expression in "boldness" suggests that one proves that he does possess it by expressing it in word and/or deed. So here also is a veiled reference to one's being involved in the world-mission.

If the uncertain hope involved in the Mosaic covenant of works entailed a responsibility, how much more so under the Abrahamic or Christian covenant of grace—a guaranteed hope! So the Christian does not need to be concerned about the abiding nature of his justification. He does not work to secure or assure it. He should work for Christ because he does have this assurance. In Ephesians 2:8–10 regeneration is not out of man or his work as the source. It is out of God by grace through faith. But it should result in good works. "For we are his workmanship, created [God's work] in Christ Jesus unto [*epi,* upon, goal, result] good works, which God hath before ordained that we should walk in them" (v.10).

3. The Reference to History (3:7–11)

The author now moved more fully into the Exodus epic to call his readers to faithfulness in the world-mission. In doing this he began with an extended quotation from Psalm 95:7–11. The psalmist introduces this passage with the words "For he is our God; and we are the people of his pasture, and the sheep of his hand" (v.7). As God's sheep he has the right to expect a yield from them in wool and mutton. The Hebrew Christians are such people, such sheep from which God has the right to expect spiritual service. It is the Father's will to give the kingdom to his "little flock" (Luke 12:32). But he wills to use them in establishing it in men's hearts.

Wherefore as the Holy Ghost [Spirit] saith, Today if ye will hear his voice, harden not your hearts, as in the provocation, in the day of temptation in the wilderness: when your fathers tempted me, proved me, and saw my works forty years (vv.7–9). The call to fidelity like that of Moses and especially that of Christ entails the possibility of failure. Hence this warning drawn from the past history of God's people. This is introduced by the word **wherefore** (v.7). It is related directly to the words **harden not your hearts** (v.8).

The verb rendered **harden** means to dry up, to become hard or stiff. When they hear God's voice calling them to their task, they are not to do this, the heart suggesting the will. God's will is expressed in his call, and it should not fall upon hard hearts or stubborn wills. Although the word "hearts" is used, each heart must decide for itself.

As in the provocation, suggests the historical event when the people of Israel hardened their hearts to Jehovah's call. The provocation is described as **the day of temptation [trial, testing] in the wilderness.** The provocation and testing are related. In the Hebrew text of Psalm 95:8 these read *Meribah* and *Massah*. Robertson refers these to Exodus 17:1–7 where at Rephidim the people complained because of a lack of water. Moses at Jehovah's command struck the rock and water came forth. So Moses called the place Meribah and Massah (v.7).

However, in Hebrews 3:9 the author relates the experience to the entire period of forty years from the exodus to the entering into the land of Canaan.[6] "When your fathers tempted [tested, tried] me, proved me, and saw my works forty-years." Note that they put God to the test and found him genuine. He was worthy of their trust. So the historical reference was not to one event but to this entire period. It should be noted that the Septuagint from which the author quoted does not use the names Meribah and Massah but *parapikrasmos* (embitterment, exasperation) and *peirasmos* (temptation, testing, trial), the words found in Hebrews 3:8. And since God cannot be *tempted* to do evil, the meanings of testing or trial apply here. Certainly the Israelites were bitter and exasperating as they put Jehovah to the test.

Wherefore I was grieved with that generation, and said, They do alway err in their heart; and they have not known my ways. So I sware in my wrath, They shall not enter into my rest (vv. 10–11).

The word rendered **grieved** means extreme anger and disgust. In the New Testament it is found only here and in verse 17. This was Jehovah's attitude toward the first generation out of Egypt. The author implied that this should not happen to his generation of readers. Their forefathers erred or wandered astray from Jehovah's will, failing to understand his ways with them or his purpose for them. So in his abiding wrath *(orgē)* God took an oath that they should not enter his **rest** or the land of Canaan (see chapter 4).

Notice the word for **wrath** *(orgē)*. *Thumos* expresses a sudden outburst of anger which soon subsides (cf. the destruction of Sodom). But *orgē* connotes God's abiding opposition to evil (cf. Rom. 1:18; also Matt. 3:7). It was this wrath which resulted in Israel's failure. It is God's abiding opposition to all rebellion against God and his will. And the mention of "rest" relates it to one definite event in the forty year period.

4. The Second Exhortation (3:12–15)

So at this point the author made his second exhortation to his readers. And note that it deals directly with an event in the Exodus epic. **Take heed, brethren, lest there be in any of you an evil heart of unbelief, in departing from the living God** (v.12).

Note **the living God** as a phrase used to differentiate between the true God and idols. But does it not also suggest that he is the same God, still living, against whom Israel rebelled in the wilderness?

This is a solemn warning indeed. That is why the author used the word *blepete*, **take heed**, but more likely it should read, "Beware" or "Look out!" Do not let what happened to Israel happen to you! Now to what event does this warning refer? Where was it that God said that that generation should not enter into his "rest" or Canaan? It was at Kadesh-barnea (cf. Num. 13:26—14:42). It is from this event that one can best understand this exhortation. This is important because upon one's understanding of this rests the interpretation of much of Hebrews. It is vital to know exactly what the author had in mind.

In order to do this it is necessary at this point to review some history. Israel was in the bondage of Egypt, a bondage which the author saw as corresponding to his readers' former bondage to sin. Through his "apostle" Moses God had effected her redemption out of bondage and from death because of her faith in the blood of the paschal lamb (Ex. 12). At Sinai this redeemed people had entered into a covenant to be God's priest-nation to the rest of the world (Ex. 19:1–6). To carry out this mission she was to be led into the land of Canaan which would be her base of operations in carrying out the covenant.

Two years after Israel's redemption from Egypt God told Moses to send twelve spies, one from each tribe, to spy out the land of Canaan (cf. Ex. 13:1 ff.). Upon their return to Kadesh-barnea all agreed that it was a wonderful land (cf. Ex. 13:26 ff.), but they also spoke of its walled cities and giant-sized inhabitants. Nevertheless, Caleb urged Israel to move in and conquer the land. But ten of the spies said, "We be not able to go against the people; for they are stronger than we" (v.31).

The people hearkened to the ten spies (Ex. 14:1 ff.). They had rather have remained in Egypt or died in the wilderness than to die trying to conquer Canaan. They even sought to get another leader in Moses' place to lead them back into

Egypt (bondage), preferring slavery to freedom with danger.

At this point Joshua joined with Caleb saying, "If the Lord delight in us, then he will bring you into this land, and give it us . . . only rebel ye not against the Lord. . . . the Lord is with us: fear ye not" (vv.8 f.) Note the word "rebel."

Just as the people were about to kill the two spies with stones, the Lord in his glory appeared in the tabernacle saying to Moses, "How long will this people provoke [note "provocation"] me, and how long ere they believe me, for all the signs which I have shewed among them?" He said that he would smite them with pestilence, disinherit them, and raise up a new people for his purpose.

At this point Moses, the "apostle" now turned *high priest* as he interceded with Jehovah on behalf of the people (vv. 13 ff.). Finally, Jehovah said, "I have pardoned according to thy word" (v.20). However, he said that only Caleb and Joshua of that generation would enter Canaan. As for the rest, "Your carcasses shall fall in this wilderness; and all that were numbered of you . . . from twenty years old and upward . . . doubtless ye shall not come into the land." It was thus that Jehovah took an oath that they should not enter into Canaan, his "rest."

In summary, Israel rebelled against God. She wanted to return to her *unredeemed state* but could not. She had been redeemed by God's act alone, and it could not be undone. Rather, that generation would wander and die in the wilderness, so symbolic of a lost opportunity and a wasted life.

It is against this background that one should approach Hebrews 3:12. The author addressed his readers as **brethren,** Christians, a people redeemed from sin. He warned them against having **an evil heart of unbelief** which would express itself **in departing from the living God.** An evil heart may also read a "sick heart" or "will." And its sickness is unbelief.

Two words call for special attention: **unbelief** *(apistias)* and **departing** *(apostēnai).* Unfortunately, the tendency is to interpret the English words rather than the Greek words which they translate.

The Greek word for "faith" is *pistia.* The *alpha* placed before a Greek word, (alpha privative) gives it the opposite meaning. So *apistia* means "no faith." It does not mean to un-believe or to renounce a faith already held. It means not to have faith. It refers not to a past faith accepted and then rejected. It means a lack of faith in the future events.

In Numbers 14:11 Jehovah did not ask, "How long before you will renounce your past faith?" Instead, "How long will it be ere they believe me?" Their redemption out of Egypt was no longer a matter of *faith*. It was a *fact* of experience. Their problem related not to the past but the future. Despite God's many "signs" or miracles on their behalf (e.g. plagues, passover, crossing of the sea, water out of a rock), they still did not believe that he could lead them into the land of Canaan.

Now apply this to the readers of Hebrews. They had been redeemed from sin. That was a fact of past experience. But because of persecution (10:32 ff.; 12:4) and a lack of development (5:12 ff.) they were failing to enter their rest or to fulfil their place in God's world-mission. This was not due to a loss of past faith. Even though some, like Israel, had considered returning to Judaism, they could not undo their redemption. For that was by God's grace. They were held in his hands (cf. John 10:29). Their problem was a lack of faith in God's power to use them in his world-mission. And they were in danger of losing their opportunity, of "being flowed by" in God's redemptive mission for all men. So their problem was not that of losing a faith once held, but of having no faith in God for enabling them to achieve their destiny which yet lay ahead.

What about **departing** from the living God? What is meant by *apostēnai?* It is an aorist infinitive of *aphistēmi,* to stand off from, to step aside from. In this context (3:12) it is usually regarded in the sense of *apostasy* which involves the loss of salvation. But apostasy is not a translation of the meaning found in the Greek word *apostasia.* Rather, it is a transliteration which carries an entirely different meaning. So it is not the basic meaning but a derived theological meaning. Cf. *baptizō,* submerge, immerse, and *baptism* which is given various meanings, even sprinkling or pouring.

So once again it is well to turn to the *original* Greek, the papyri. In the papyri this verb is used in the sense of repelling invaders, renouncing a claim to or give up occupation of.[7] It is used in the sense of revolt in Acts 5:37. It is used in the Septuagint to translate the idea of revolt in Ezekiel 20:8.

In the papyri its derivatives are used for revolt or rebellion. *Apostatēs* is also used in the same sense. Plutarch used it in the sense of political revolt. Arndt and Gingrich define *apostasia* as rebellion, citing Joshua 22:22, "if it be in rebellion." So Acts 21:21 may read, "Rebellion you teach from Moses." It is clear then that one is justified in seeing the basic idea in *apostēnai* as that of renouncing a claim, rebellion or revolt.[8]

And these ideas fit the action of Israel at Kadesh-barnea. When Jehovah proposed to lead her into Canaan, she stood off or aside from him. She rebelled or revolted against his authority and leadership (cf. Num. 14:9). In so doing she renounced her claim to the covenant relationship. She refused to occupy the land of her destiny. Even though she considered returning to Egypt, the state of bondage from which she had been redeemed, she could not do so. Jehovah did threaten punishment and disinheritance from the covenant, but at Moses' plea he did not do either. Rather that generation lost its opportunity of performing in the covenant, a privilege which was extended to another generation. That rebellious generation did not enter into her "rest" (cf. chapter 4).

This same fate awaited the readers of this epistle if they rebelled against the living God in refusing to become an active part of his world-mission. There is no thought here of losing their salvation. Apostasy in the popular sense does not apply. Or else this verse runs head-on against the general tenor of New Testament teachings. But they are in danger of revolting against the missionary commissions or renouncing their own covenant relation with Christ.

Someone objected to this interpretation. To him the warnings here and elsewhere throughout the epistle were too severe for such a meaning. But think of the souls that would be lost from Christ if this rebellion continued. That is crime enough to call for God's wrath. And seen in eternal values, the loss of this opportunity takes on dire and infinite proportions. The world is in its present condition because Christ's people have so largely rebelled against the Great Commission.

But exhort one another daily, while it is called Today; lest any of you be hardened through the deceitfulness of sin (v.13).

On the positive side the author called on his readers to exhort or encourage each other daily to be faithful in their calling. **While** [so long as] **it is called Today** could mean so long as God is calling the readers to faithfulness, or while their opportunity remained. Westcott suggests the sense as until the second coming of Christ or so long as the readers lived. Could it not also refer to *opportunity* so long as or while they have opportunity to respond. Certainly God is calling them while they live, and will do so until he says that it is enough in the Lord's return.

They should not allow their hearts or wills to be hardened by the deceitfulness of sin. **Deceitfulness** may be rendered trick or defraud. Sin, or Satan, is aggressive to trick them into rebellion against God's will and to defraud them of their opportunity in God's world-mission.

For we are made partakers of Christ, if we hold the beginning of our confidence stedfast unto the end (v.14).

Something of the thought of verse 6 is repeated in verse 14. Literally, "For we have become [perfect tense of completed action] partners [*metochoi,* see 3:1] of Christ, if we possess the beginning of the pledged profession [substance] unto the end guaranteed." **The beginning** suggests an original experience which continues to grow and develop. It probably refers to the experience of regeneration followed immediately by sanctification, a state in which the believer is to fulfil God's purpose for his Christian life. This thought is also present in the *pledged profession.* If one possesses this experience he is a partner of Christ in God's redemptive mission. It is not a matter of losing one's salvation if he does not hold on to it. It is a matter of really having it—guaranteed unto the end—and showing it by his conduct. The form of conditional sentence here, as in verse 6, contains doubt as to whether the readers really possess it. If they do, then they are Christ's partners and should act like such.

So the author ended his exhortation by citing again the vital importance of responding positively to the call of God to world-mission (v.15). It is only thus that the Christian can fulfil the reason for his being.

5. The Summary of Warning (3:16–19)

The author called upon his readers to look again at Israel's experience at Kadesh-barnea. Some of the Israelites, indeed all but three twenty years old and above, did provoke God by refusing to enter Canaan.

Howbeit not all that came out of Egypt by Moses (v.16). This refers especially to Caleb and Joshua. And they alone of all twenty years old and above were privileged to enter the land of promise. Which suggests that each reader is challenged to decide the matter for himself. Though all others may miss their opportunity, those who have faith in God's will can seize theirs.

But with whom was he grieved forty years? was it not with them that had sinned, whose carcases fell in the wilderness? And to whom sware he that they should not enter into his rest, but to them that believed not? (vv. 17–18).

Who were the ones who died in the wilderness without ever reaching Canaan? It was those **that believed not.** Actually, **believed not** here renders the word meaning to be disobedient. Through their rebellion at Kadesh-barnea they were deprived of the privilege. As a result they wandered for thirty-eight years in a barren wilderness and died there.

So we see that they could not enter in because of unbelief (*apistias,* v.19). It was through no faith (cf. v.12). It was not a past faith disavowed but a future faith not expressed or exercised. So the idea of apostasy in the popular sense does not apply here. It is not the loss of a past experience. It is the loss of a future opportunity. And the reason was "no faith."

Christians who are disobedient or who rebel through no faith in God to lead them in a successful world-mission likewise lose their opportunity. One may have a saved soul but a wasted life. It is no wonder that the author began his exhortation to Christian duty with the word "Beware!" Beware lest they have an evil heart of *no faith* in God's ability to lead them in the accomplishment of their world-mission for Him.

Notes

1. *Op. cit.,* p. 74.
2. For a lengthy discussion of these words see Hobbs, *op. cit.,* pp. 92–96.
3. *Op. cit.;* cf. Neil, *op. cit.,* p. 45; Grant, *op. cit.,* p. 26; Manson, *op. cit.,* p. 52; Schneider, *op. cit.,* p. 25.
4. Hobbs, *op. cit.,* pp. 33–36.
5. Moulton and Milligan, *op. cit.,* pp. 336 f.
6. Cf. Westcott, *op. cit.,* p. 82.
7. See also Arndt and Gingrich, *op. cit.,* p. 126.
8. Hobbs, *op. cit.,* pp. 25–29.

IV. The Call to Duty

In Hebrews 3 the author spoke repeatedly of a "rest." In chapter 4 he explained what he meant by it, and he urged his readers to enter into it as they relied on Jesus to enable them to do so.

1. The Promised Rest (4:1-3)

This is a poor chapter division. For the author did not take up a new idea. Instead he continued his exhortation begun in chapter 3. He had urged his readers to enter into their *rest.* Now he called on them to be fearful lest they should fail to do so.

Let us therefore fear, lest, a promise being left us of entering into his rest, any of you should seem to come short of it (v.1).

The Israelites lost their opportunity because of no faith. The same danger threatened these Hebrew Christians, as indeed, it does every generation of believers. God had promised this land of rest, but his people are responsible for seizing it. The promise still holds for those who will receive it.

What is meant by **rest?** The word so translated *(katapausin)* means a place of rest or a cessation of labor. Arndt and Gingrich (p. 416) calls it "stopping, causing to rest." The verb is used of God resting on the seventh day (cf. Gen. 2:2). In Exodus 31:18 it is translated "made an end." Moulton and Milligan (p. 331) list under the verb *katapauo (katapaustikos)* the sense of a musical rest.

But how did the author of Hebrews use the word for rest? In this chapter his first use is in verse 4 where it refers to God's rest at the end of his creative work. His second use is in verse 5 where it refers to the rest promised to the children of Israel. But he made a distinction in rest between verses 8-9. The meaning becomes clear as these passages are examined.

But in verse 1 the author urged his readers to enter into this rest lest they should **come short** of it. This translates the verb *hustereō,* meaning to come too late, fail to reach, to miss a goal or to be excluded from something. Arndt and Gingrich (p. 856) cites these as the meaning in Hebrews 4:1. It is also used in the sense of lacking, being inferior, or coming short of a goal.

It would appear, therefore, that one must look beyond the usual idea of apostasy for the meaning of rest. It must be interpreted in the light of 3:12 ff., as one keeps in mind the author's allegorical interpretation of the Exodus epic.

The warning, therefore, is that the readers, like Israel, should fail to reach, fall short of their goal, of being inferior, lacking, and, therefore, excluded from God's purpose. It expresses the idea resident in being flowed by (cf. 2:1).

For unto us was the gospel preached, as well as unto them: but the word preached did not profit them, not being mixed with faith to them that heard it (v.2).

The word **gospel** should not be limited to the plan of regeneration. It should be read in the light of God's covenant with Israel. Thus it relates primarily to sanctification and ultimately to glorification. In the author's mind Israel at Sinai was a *redeemed* people. They had believed the "gospel" about God's deliverance from Egyptian bondage, and through their faith they had been redeemed out of it. **The word preached** which did not profit them was the *good tidings* of God's covenant to make this redeemed people a priest-nation to the rest of the world. This was a gospel indeed, that they should be partners with God in so great an undertaking. But their opportunity in it depended upon their being true to this covenant. At Kadesh-barnea they had renounced it in their rebellion. So they were "not united [mixed] by faith with the one's hearing." In this case with Caleb and Joshua who honored the covenant.

Us refers to the author and his Hebrew-Christian readers. They also were a redeemed people. And they were a covenant people, partners with Christ in the heavenly calling. The gospel to them is the good news that they have been chosen to have a place in God's world-mission. But this word will profit them only as they are in faith united with those who respond to this privilege. Thus this gospel is primarily with respect to sanctification with an ultimate view toward glorification.

For we which have believed do enter into rest, as he said, As I have sworn in my wrath, if they shall enter into my rest: although the works were finished from the foundation of the world (v.3)

Do enter is an emphatic futuristic present middle indicative form (Robertson). As it was those who had no faith who did not enter into Canaan and those with faith who did, so it is with regard to the Hebrew Christians. Only those who believe in Christ to empower them for their world-mission shall enter "into rest" (cf. 3:11).

God's redemptive work in his heart was finished *(genēthentōn,* from *ginomai,* to become) before the creation of the world. Now it had been wrought out in history (cf. 10:55 ff.; Rev. 13:8). God's work through the Son had been finished. The redemptive mission henceforth depended upon his people. It was into this "rest" that the author called his readers. So he proceeded to explain it.

2. The Rest of God (4:4–5)

For he spoke in a certain place of the seventh day on this wise, And God did rest the seventh day from all his works. And in this place again, If they shall enter into my rest (vv. 4–5).

The author based the "rest" of God upon his own rest from his creative work.

But as will be seen in 4:9 this rest looked beyond the moment to a different kind of rest. The author's scriptural reference is to Genesis 2:2. "And God did rest the seventh day from all his works" (v.4). It should be noted, however, that **all** renders *pantōn* without the definite article. It refers to God's works in their several parts, not to his work as a whole.

That from which God rested, of course, was his creative work. The word for "rest" is *katapausis*. This does not mean that he was tired. It simply means that he ceased his creative activity. For he continued to work in other ways (cf. v.9). This certainly does not point to the "land of rest" (heaven) about which Christians used to sing. For even there God's people shall serve him but without becoming weary.

Furthermore, the author cited God's promise to his people, **If they shall enter into my rest** (v.5; cf. 3:11,18; 4:3). God's rest was to cease his act of creation but to continue other kinds of work. It follows, therefore, that the promise of "my rest" to his people is a similar cessation of work. For the author used the same word *katapausis*. God's work, up to the point of his rest, actually produced the condition in which he would continue to work.

Now, in this light, how may one regard the "rest" into which God's people are to enter? The writer sees it as Israel's entrance into and taking the land of Canaan. Thus she would cease her work to possess it. But it was from this land that she was to carry out her world-mission as a priest-nation. Therefore she rested from one thing to begin doing another. This land had been promised to Abraham and his seed for this very purpose.

An examination of a map of the ancient world will explain why. Modern people are prone to see Palestine as an out-of-the-way place. But it was at the heart of the ancient world. A land bridge between the Mediterranean sea and the desert, it joined together the continents of Africa, Asia, and Europe. The highways of the nations ran through Palestine. So from this vantage point the priest-nation could touch the ancient empires of the world as their traders, couriers, and armies moved from one continent to another.

But before Israel could begin this covenant work she must enter and subdue it. And that she refused to do at Kadesh-barnea. Note that the word is "If they shall enter into my rest."

Now in the author's mind how did this correspond to his readers? At present they were in a state of failing to enter into that rest. Whatever may be the reason (persecution, dwelling under the shadow of Judaism, or simply an arrested development) they were not filling their place in God's world-mission. To do so required struggle. They must dedicate and prepare themselves before they could be used of God in it. Once they had done this they would "rest" or cease that labor to begin another or actually to do that for which they were called. They had accepted God's elected plan of redemption for themselves. But they were rejecting the position of being his elected people to propagate that plan. Hence the "if they shall enter into my rest" or cessation from the work of preparing to begin the work of propagation.

3. The Obligation of God's People (4:6-7)

It remaineth that some must enter therein, and they to whom it was first preached entered not in because of their unbelief (v.6).

The promise still abides. This is the meaning of **remaineth** (*apoleipō*, to remain over). Those who received the first "gospel" to be a priest-nation did not enter because of *disobedience* (cf. 3:18, "believed not" and "unbelief" here). This was due to their rebellion at Kadesh-barnea (cf. 3:12, 19). Now under the Christian covenant the Hebrew-Christians are a part of the new "chosen generation, a royal priesthood, an holy nation, a peculiar people" (1 Peter 2:9). And the same gospel is preached to them. They are to fill their place in God's world-mission in spite of the first priest-nation's rebellion.

Again, he limiteth a certain day, saying in David, Today, after so long a time; as it said, Today if ye will hear his voice, harden not your hearts (v.7).

The call to Israel did not end at Kadesh-barnea. It came again and again through the centuries. In David's words in Psalm 95:7-8 it came again. The word **limiteth** renders *horizō*, to mark out boundaries (note "horizon") or to define. So through David God defined this **today**, the day of decision as at Kadesh-barnea. God's purpose continued, and he called for his people to fill their place in it.

Now under the new covenant the call comes loud and clear. In the very land which God had chosen he had in Jesus Christ wrought out his historical redemptive work. And he expects his people, beginning in Jerusalem and Judea, to go throughout the earth discipling all nations (cf. Acts 1:8; Matt. 28:18-20). One's Jerusalem and Judea is where he is at the moment. And if he is truly a partner in the gospel, God calls him to be about the work of his redemptive mission.

4. The Rest of God's People (4:8-10)

The fact of the matter is that the "rest" which God had in mind for Israel was an incomplete one. This reminds the readers that that to which they are called is greater than that to which Israel was called. Thus the rest of the Christian is *better* than that of Israel. This is another note of the superiority of the new covenant over the old.

For if Jesus had given them rest, then would he not afterward have spoken of another day (v.8). **Jesus** *(Iēsous)* is the Greek equivalent of the Hebrew *Yeshua* or Joshua. So the context here calls for "Joshua," not "Jesus."

With this verse the author went beyond Kadesh-barnea to the actual entrance into Canaan of the next generation of Israel under Joshua. But even this was an incomplete **rest.** For one thing, Israel failed to rid the land of the Canaanites as God had told her. As a result Israel became paganized by her neighbors rather than leading them to worship Jehovah. Israel soon lost her sense of mission in her own ambition for worldly power and glory (cf. 1 Sam. 8). The remainder of her history as a nation is a sad story of such. Even her pride in her covenant relation led her to despise the very people to whom she was to minister, and she was despised in turn.

Had Israel fulfilled her mission, there would have been no need for God through David to point to **another day.** It was this very failure which caused the author to warn his readers against hardening their wills against God's call to them (cf. 3:7–8).

There remaineth therefore a rest to the people of God (v.9). But notice that the author used a different word for **rest** here. The word is *sabbatismos!* A sabbath-kind-of-rest.

This is the only time that this word appears in the New Testament. Moffatt notes an uncertain use of it in Plutarch.[1] Robertson calls it a "doubtful passage in Plutarch." In all likelihood this is its only occurrence in Greek literature. Moulton and Milligan list no use of it in the papyri or inscriptions, noting that it was probably coined by the author.[2] Moffatt and Robertson agree with this. The verb is found in the Septuagint in Exodus 16:30.

However, Robertson says that here *sabbatismos* is parallel with *katapausis.* If that be true why would the author have gone to the trouble of coining a word to say the same thing? Evidently the author did this in order to bring out a contrast in meaning.

Moffatt also sees *sabbatismos* as synonymous with *katapausis.* " 'Rest' throughout all this passage—and the writer never refers to it again—is the blissful existence of God's faithful in the next world." [3] If this be the meaning, then it is also the sense that one can have redemption and later lose it.[4] Of course, Moffatt's statement makes the entire discussion in chapters 3—4 eschatological —or to refer to glorification. This eschatological thought is an ultimate meaning. But the weight of evidence is against the idea of having and losing redemption.

Thomas seems to be nearer to what the author was saying. Talking about *katapausis* he says:

But in this passage [4:3] the predominant thought is not rest of conscience through redemption, but rest of the heart through surrender and obedience. The believer is regarded as already out of Egypt and journeying toward Canaan. "The danger is not lest the blood should not be on the lintel, but lest we should break down by the way, as thousands did in the wilderness . . . When he speaks of rest, it is the rest of the kingdom he talks of, not the rest of the conscience" (*Musings on Hebrews,* by J. B. Bellett).[5]

Then on *sabbatismos* he adds.

The word "rest" is suddenly and it would seem significantly changed, and instead of the ordinary word, it means "Sabbath rest;" but the primary idea is concerned with the present and not with the future, with the believer's life here and now, and only with Heaven as the completing and culminating point, the thought of "the Sabbath of the soul" in fellowship with God . . . This means not the absence of activity, but that harmony of soul within which produces loyalty of character and conduct; and just as God ceased working after Creation, so also, when we enter into spiritual rest, we cease from our striving, because, as our attitude is one of confidence in God, we are in harmony with His will.[6]

However, even this does not seem to satisfy the author's change from *katapausis* to *sabbatismos*. The former denotes God's rest from creation. But did God cease to *work* at that point? The Bible says that he did not, to say nothing about nature. God ceased his creative work, but he continues his providential work. More to the point in Hebrews, God continues his redemptive work.

Immediately upon the finish of his work in creation, God began his work of redemption (Gen. 3:15). He was working at it in his charge to Abraham (Gen. 12), in the redemption of Israel from Egypt, and he was seeking to perform it through the promised *rest* of Israel in Canaan. It was this work of the Father which Jesus was doing in John 5 and in all his incarnate experience [including Calvary, II Cor. 5:19]. It was this same work which God was seeking to do through the Hebrew Christians whom he had already redeemed from bondage and death.[7]

It is in this light that the writer sees *sabbatismos* as the Sabbath-kind-of-rest which God had following his *katapausis* from creation. And applying it to the Hebrew Christians, it is their redemptive world-mission after they have finished their *katapausis* of dedication and preparation for that service. After Israel arrived in Canaan there still remained the covenant work as a priest-nation. The author urged his readers to enter their Canaan that they may carry out their new covenant in God's world-mission. This thought is borne out in verse 10.

For he that is entered into his rest [*katapausin*], **he** [*autos*, emphatic in comparison with God] **also hath ceased** [*katepausen*] **from his own works** [of getting ready to witness], **as God** [emphatic] **did from his** (v.10). It certainly involves a character "in harmony with His will" (Thomas), but it is one that will be found filling its place in God's world-mission.

5. The Admonition to Faithfulness (4:11–13)

Let us labour therefore to enter into his rest, lest any man fall after the same example of unbelief (v.11).

The author continued his exhortation to faithfulness on the part of his readers. Because God has designed a *sabbatismos* for his people, they should **labour** to enter into the *katapausis* in order that they may carry out his will. "Labour" renders a volitive aorist subjunctive of *spoudazō*, to hasten, to be eager and alert. The aorist tense calls for an immediate exercise of the will in this regard. This it to prevent anyone from falling according to the same example of **unbelief** or "disobedience" (*apeitheias;* cf. 3:18; 4:6).

God's promise to give this rest is sure. But he also detects any failure to enter into it. No Christian can escape the probing and revealing power of his word. This is true in this case or in any other.

For the word of God is quick, and powerful, and sharper than any two-edged sword, piercing even to the dividing asunder of soul and spirit, and of the joints and marrow, and is a discerner of the thoughts and intents of the heart (v.12).

Quick means "living" *(zōn)*. In the Greek text this comes first, and so is emphatic. It is not a dead word out of the past. It is the living word of the living

God. And it is personified in Jesus Christ. So it is very much alive to the Christian. This word in Him is the final, full revelation of God (cf. 1:2). He is the living expression of God's spoken word. His command is final and abiding.

Furthermore, this word is **powerful** or active and energetic. It is more cutting or **sharper** than any doubled bladed or "two-mouthed" sword which cuts both ways. Carrying out the idea of the sword, it is **piercing** (old verb for "going through"), even to the dividing **of soul and spirit, and of joints and marrow.** But the sword becomes a surgeon's knife. The idea is that God's word lays bare, opens up the inner-most elements of man's being. It even judges with regard to **the thoughts and intents of the heart.**

The figure is that of a surgeon opening up one's body to discover and remove diseased organs and tissue. He goes to the very heart of the matter. God's word lays bare man's innermost being even to the lurking doubts and evils—rebellion —in the heart or will.

Neither is there any creature [not even a germ] **that is not manifest in his sight: but all things are naked and opened unto the eyes of him with whom we have to do** (v.13).

The author unknowingly anticipated the most powerful microscope able to see things not visible to the natural eye. "Not even one thing" *(panta)* is hidden from God. Each individual element is laid bare. It is **opened** to him. This translates the perfect tense (completeness) of the verb *trachēlizō*. (Note the English word "tracheotomy.") This verb connotes the idea of bending back the neck as a surgeon does in an operation. God sees all of one's inmost thoughts. **With whom we have to do** reads literally, "to whom is our account."

In other words the Christian must answer to God, one who knows all about him. No one can hide from Him his secret motives and thoughts. In this case it had to do with faith or lack of it, obedience to or rebellion against God's will in his plan for the readers' lives. Certainly they could not plead ignorance. And they could not cover their failure under false pretenses. For this reason the author urged them to be faithful and obedient.

6. The Christian's Reliance (4:14–16)

In his struggle to be faithful the Christian has an ally on whom he may rely. It is one who Himself faced the struggle and won the victory. He does not ask his people to do what he has not done.

Seeing then that we have a great high priest, that is passed into the heavens, Jesus the Son of God, let us hold fast our profession (v.14). Here the author took up the matter of Jesus' high priesthood to which he had alluded previously (cf. 1:3; 2:17 f.; 3:1). This will be at the center of his message through 12:3.

Under the old covenant the high priest annually passed into the Holy of Holies, where God was said to dwell in mercy with his people, to accomplish an atonement for the sins of the people. Thus they were cleansed and made fit for God's service. The High Priest of the new covenant entered into heaven itself, into the very presence of God, to atone for their sins. Thus they are sanctified unto God's service.

Note that he is **Jesus the Son of God.** The author combined his human and divine names. He perfectly represents both man and God as the perfect Mediator (cf. 1 Tim. 2:5). It is through him that Christians are purged or purified as instruments in God's service.

The word rendered **hold fast** *(krateō)* means to seize or grasp with power. Its resultant sense is to hold on and not let go. In their profession the readers have entered into a covenant relation with Jesus Christ. They are not to deny that covenant through rebellion. Rather they are to hold on to it with power as though their very lives depended upon it. Not their redemption but their sanctification and, ultimately, their glorification. They are through obedience to enter their "Canaan" that they may discharge their obligation under their covenant.

For we have not an high priest which cannot be touched with the feeling of our infirmities; but was in all points tempted like as we are, yet without sin (v.15).

This High Priest is not one who is "not able to sympathize with our weaknesses." This is because he has shared in the temptations which are endured by his people. **Tempted** renders a perfect passive participle which expresses the completeness of Jesus' temptation brought to him by Satan. He endured the same temptations as do his people.

This is the very essence of Jesus' complete identity with man "apart from sin" or sinning. Which raises the question as to whether or not Jesus could have yielded to temptation. The answer must be in the affirmative or else his temptations were not real. If the latter be true then he merely pretended to be tempted, which would be hypocrisy—the sin he condemned unmercifully (cf. Matt. 23).

Some object to this idea that Jesus could have yielded to temptation, saying that God cannot be tempted with evil (cf. Jas. 1:13). It should be remembered, however, that Jesus was *human* as well as *divine.* It is as great an error to deny the former as the latter. In his temptation experience in Matthew 4 (cf. Luke 4) Jesus was tempted in his humanity; he resisted in his humanity. Not once did he call on his divine power to resist the devil. He depended upon prayer and meditation, a complete dedication to God's will, the Scriptures, and the power of the Holy Spirit. Each of these is available to every Christian.

Luke 4:13 speaks of "all the temptation" or "every single kind of temptation" *(panta peirasmon). Panta* without the definite article singles out each one. This same word is used in Hebrews 4:15. "Having been tempted according to each one" *(panta).*

Satan tempts man in his higher nature, not his lower. He seeks to get him to express legitimate desires in an illegitimate way. Actually he tempts man in his physical appetite, aesthetic nature, and ambition. These are seen in Genesis 3:6 (cf. Matt. 4:3,6,9). He caught Eve but failed on Jesus.

It is also objected that Jesus had no sinful nature or antecedent sins. True. But a comparison between Adam and Jesus is most revealing. Adam was created in a state of innocence. He could be neither righteous nor unrighteous until he had a choice between God's will and Satan's will. Subsequent events showed that while innocent he had a tendency toward sin. He fell and the race fell with him.

In regard to his temptations Jesus as the representative Man was also in a state of innocence as to God's will for his life. He was offered a choice between God's will and Satan's will. He had a tendency toward righteousness. So he chose God's will. And in his victory all men may share through faith in him.

Yes, Jesus had the power to sin. But more gloriously he had the power not to sin. So he was tempted in each single area of temptation (physical appetite, aesthetic nature, and ambition) **yet without sin.**

With regard to this present passage it is of interest to note that his temptations in the wilderness and beyond (cf. Matt. 16:21 ff.; 27:39 ff.; John 6:14 f.) were with respect to his role in God's redemptive purpose. It is for this reason that he is able to sympathize with and help Christians as they are tempted to revolt against God's will regarding their place in the world-mission. No one knows the power of temptation like one who has endured it fully and won the battle. Jesus has done this. So he is the sympathetic High Priest to help all who are tempted.

Let us therefore come boldly unto the throne of grace, that we may obtain mercy, and find grace to help in time of need (v.16). The present tense means to keep on coming or to do so from time to time when temptation assails. Rather than to rebel, come to him who can give victory. Because Jesus is at God's throne it is one of grace. And the author says to come **boldly** or with boldness. Since this great High Priest has passed through the heavenly veil, each Christian in him has access with no need to fear.

Regeneration is by grace. But grace also extends in all experiences of the Christian life. John 1:16 reads, "And of his fulness have all we received, and grace for grace." Or grace following after grace. Like manna in the wilderness, there is a new supply available every day, yea, for every new trial. So when he is tempted to rebel against God's will, the believer should come with boldness to the throne of grace. There from his sympathetic High Priest he will receive **mercy.** And find **grace to help in time of need.** Literally, "well-timed help." As Robertson says, " 'For help in the nick of time,' before too late."

God's help was available at Kadesh-barnea (cf. Num. 14:9). Nevertheless, Israel rebelled. The author did not want that to happen to the new Israel. And his exhortation applies to God's people anywhere, anytime. May it not happen today!

Notes

1. *The International Critical Commentary,* "Hebrews," Scribner's, New York, 1924, p. 53.
2. *Op. cit.,* p. 567.
3. *Op. cit.,* p. 53.
4. Schneider, *op. cit.,* pp. 30 f.
5. *Op. cit.,* p. 48.
6. *Ibid,* pp. 49 f.
7. Hobbs, *Studies in Hebrews,* Sunday School Board, Southern Baptist Convention, Nashville, 1954, p. 41.

V. The Sin of Immaturity

After 4:11 the author did not use the word "rest." But it is certainly the background against which one must understand Hebrews 5–6. He continued to discuss reasons for Israel's and his readers' failure to enter into this rest. The point of chapter 5 is the immaturity of his readers. And it is all the more inexcusable because of the work of their sympathetic and faithful High Priest.

1. The High Priesthood of Christ (5:1–6)

It has been noted that the function of the high priest on the Day of Atonement was to purify Israel, thus making the people fit vessels for God's service. The author showed by comparison that Christ is a superior High Priest. Two things were essential for anyone to be a high priest. He must have human sympathy and a divine appointment. These things are discussed in verses 1–4.

For every high priest taken from among men is ordained for man in things pertaining to God, that he may offer both gifts and sacrifices for sins (v.1).

Under the Mosaic system the high priest was taken "out of [*ek*] men . . . on behalf of [*huper*] men." He was one of his fellows chosen of God to minister in the tabernacle on their behalf. And he ministered in things pertaining to God or "the things before [*pros*] God." **May offer** renders *prosphero*, used of bearing an offering to God before the altar.

Gifts and sacrifices suggests the whole of the offering system in which the sacrifices preceded the other offerings, such as the meal offering. But the author's idea is primarily with regard to the Day of Atonement which in his mind embodied the entire sacrificial system. Even when other priests presided in the day to day offerings they acted under and/or for the high priest.

For sins means as a substitute for sins. The sacrifice was made that the victim might die as a substitute for the sinner. This is the meaning of "for" *(huper)*. It was used in the Septuagint in Isaiah 53:5, and of Jesus in John 10:11 (cf. 2 Cor. 5:20-21, "for," "in stead"). Of course, the high priest made the sacrifice for his own sins as well as those of the people (cf. v.3).

Who can have compassion on the ignorant, and on them that are out of the way; for that he himself also is compassed with infirmity (v.2).

Because the high priest was himself surrounded by his own weakness in sin, he was able to "bear gently" or to be compassionate toward other sinners. Here the author distinguished between sinners who were **ignorant** or without knowledge, namely, those who sinned in ignorance or unintentionally, and the "erring" or ones **out of the way**, namely, those who wandered astray deliberately. For, in fact, he offered sacrifices for his own sins as well as those of the people (v.3).

Furthermore, a high priest did not choose his position, but was chosen of God, as was Aaron (v.4). Aaron did not "run" for the position; he was called by God to fill it.

Having dealt with the high priest of Israel, the author went on to show that Christ likewise did not appoint himself as High Priest. He *was* High Priest in the will of the Father.

So also Christ glorified not himself to be made an high priest; but he that said unto him, Thou art my Son, today have I begotten thee (v.5; cf. 1:5; Psalm 2:7).

Christ did not seek the position. The Father placed it upon him. But it was eternal whereas that of Aaron was temporal. Was Christ's high priesthood co-eval (Bruce) with his Sonship? Or was it simply fitting because he was Son (Davidson)? It would be difficult to separate the two. But one thing is clear. He was not a self-made High Priest. He was appointed to the office by the Father. In this sense his office was similar to that of Aaron.

Yet it was infinitely greater. This the author showed by quoting Psalm 110:4.

Thou art a priest for ever after the order of Melchisedec (v.6). Melchisedec is mentioned in Genesis 14:18. Thus he preceded Aaron by several hundred years. He was a priest in his own order unrelated to Aaron and his order. Christ is a priest **after the order of Melchisedec** (cf. 7:1 ff.). Thus his priesthood preceded that of Aaron. **For ever** or "unto the ages" makes this fact infinite. Thus his is an eternal priesthood. It means that his priesthood is "co-eval" with his Sonship.

2. The Faithfulness of Christ (5:7)

Who in the days of his flesh, when he had offered up prayers and supplications with strong crying and tears unto him that was able to save him from death, and was heard in that he feared. In his divine appointment Christ fulfilled one requirement for high-priesthood (cf. v.4). Now the author proceeded to show his qualification through human sympathy (cf. vv.1–3).

The obvious reference is to Gethsemane. The struggle there was not between Jesus and Satan. It was a struggle within his own will that it might be one with that of the Father. **Death** involves not just physical death. For Jesus knew that was to be. Rather, it involved his becoming sin (cf. 2 Cor. 5:21) that in his death sin might receive the full wrath of God. If there were any other way, . . . but if not, God's will be done. So Jesus surrendered to the Father's will.

He was heard in that he **feared.** This means godly fear. He reverenced the Father's redemptive will and purpose, and God strengthened him for the task (cf. Lk. 22:43).

The author's inference is that it will not be easy for his readers to submit to

God's will in the world-mission. But through dedication and prayer they can receive God's power to submit to it. As their High Priest was faithful so must they be faithful.

3. The Example of Christ (5:8)

Though he were a Son, yet learned he obedience by the things which he suffered.

Sonship implies deity. But he was also human, and as such he had to learn as any other person. This is evidenced by his youth. Luke 2:52 says, "And Jesus increased in wisdom and stature, and in favour with God and man." He grew in wisdom, stature, and grace. "Increased" renders a verb meaning to cut forward. It pictures one with difficulty cutting his way through underbrush as in a jungle. The imperfect tense shows that Jesus did this continuously. He learned with the same "brain sweat" necessary for any other child.

By the same difficult process he learned obedience to God's will. True, he always did his Father's will (John 4:34; 8:29). But it was not without a struggle, as seen in his various temptations. But He **learned** *(emathen)* obedience through the things that He **suffered** *(epathen)*. Note the play on words: *emathen . . . epathen.*

These Hebrew Christians were being deterred from doing God's will because of a state of arrested development. This was due to both persecution and a lack of a sense of mission or rebellion against such. They also must learn obedience through suffering. This included persecution, but more. They must cut their way forward through their difficulties as they progress toward a knowledge of and a dedication to God's world-mission. It is not easy, then or now, but each Christian must live one day at a time with his eyes ever on the ultimate goal. Each victory over temptation gives promise of others. And gradually he shall arrive at the goal of obedience to God's will.

4. The Gift of Christ (5:9–11)

It was through his obedience learned through suffering that Christ fulfilled his mission as Redeemer. It was this fulfilment which had provided for the redemption of these Hebrew Christians. It was a gift which they did not earn. But it entailed responsibility to share it with others.

And being made perfect, he became the author of eternal salvation unto all them that obey him (v.9).

This verse refers back to Christ' qualifications as High Priest: divine appointment and human sympathy. But it looks beyond these to the accomplishment of his work as such in history. Eternally he was High Priest as he was Son. But he was made **perfect.** This translates the verb *teleioō*, to complete a process and so arrive at a goal. The process was learning through suffering. Thus Christ was made perfect or complete. The reference is not to being rid of fault but of achieving a purpose.

It was thus that he **became the author [source] of eternal salvation. Became** renders *egeneto* from *ginomai*. It means to become something that one was not previously. Thus "the Word was made [*egeneto*] flesh" (John 1:14). He became what he had not been before. In this case he became the source out of which flowed eternal salvation. In eternity Christ was destined for such. But he became it in the arena of history.

Salvation, of course, refers primarily to redemption. But it may also be seen in its fuller meaning: regeneration, sanctification, and glorification or the full salvation which God designs for his people. The readers of this epistle had been regenerated and sanctified unto God's service. But they must in that state learn obedience in preparing for and filling their place in the world-mission. This they should do, looking toward glorification—the bodily resurrection and glory and reward in heaven.

This full salvation is for those who obey God's will. **All** renders *pasin* without the definite article. It separates the human race into each individual one. Each person is regenerated as he obeys the gospel by believing in Jesus Christ. Each one regenerated is sanctified and, in that state, must obey in developing and serving in God's world-mission. Each one will be glorified according to his obedience to God's will. So this gift of Christ is to be received and appropriated by each single Christian.

Suggested here is Caleb and Joshua as over against the disobedient ones in Israel. Each Christian should do God's will within himself irrespective of what others may or may not do.

These verses carry forward the idea of the superiority of Christ's high-priesthood over that of Aaron. Aaron's ministry of purifying Israel for service had to be repeated over and over again. That which Christ provides is eternal. This brought the author to mention again Christ's office as after the order of Melchisedec (v.10). **Of whom we have many things to say, and hard to be uttered, seeing ye are dull of hearing** (v.11).

He had many things to say about this. However, he faced two difficulties. For one thing it was **hard to be uttered** (v.11), or "hard to interpretation." The verbal form is *dusermeneutos*. Note the word "hermeneutics," the science of interpretation. The idea of a high priest preceding and greater than Aaron was a difficult thing for those with a Hebrew background to grasp. And again, the readers were **dull of hearing.** This means that they were mentally slow and sluggish. They had dull minds and hearts as well as ears. The word rendered "dull" is *nothroi*, used by Plato of stupid students. This idea the author enlarged upon in verses 12–14.

5. The Failure of Christ's People (5:12–14)

Even though Christ had learned obedience through hardship in order to provide eternal salvation, these Hebrew Christians had appropriated only regeneration. Though sanctified they had made no effort to progress beyond being babes in Christ. The new birth implies continuing growth in size, knowledge, and service. "Disciple" (student) does the same. But these readers had done none of these things. Thus they were failing to fill their place in God's world-mission.

For when for the time ye ought to be teachers, ye have need that one teach you again which be the first principles of the oracles of God; and are become such as have need of milk, and not of strong meat (v.12).

For whatever reason the readers had remained spiritual infants. At the time when they should be teaching others they were still in need of being taught the **first principles** or ABC's of Christian truth. Instead of being able to eat the strong meat of Christian truth, they still must be fed a diet of milk.

A little baby is a beautiful thing. However, one who should be an adult in size and understanding, but is still as a baby, is a monstrosity. Such were these Hebrew Christians.

For every one that useth milk is unskilful in the word of righteousness: for he is a babe (v.13).

This verse explains the previous one. These spiritual babies are **unskilful in the word of righteousness.** "Unskilful" means inexperienced. Westcott notes the absence of the definite article with "word of righteousness." Thus it does not refer to the whole of Christian doctrine. It is the "teaching which deals at once with the one source of righteousness in Christ, and the means by which man is enabled to be made a partaker of it." [1] (Cf. Rom. 1:16–17.)

That they had this righteousness is evident by the fact that they were Christians (cf. 3:1). But due to their lack of development and experience they were incapable of sharing it with others. How many Christians feel a lack of ability to witness to others about Christ!

The reason is that such is **a babe,** which renders *nēpios.* Wuest sees these as "unsaved Hebrews." [2] But the point here is not whether or not they are Christians. It refers to the immature state of these "holy brethren" (3:1). *Nēpios,* according to Delitzsch, means one who is incapable of speech.[3] Arndt and Gingrich lists the basic meaning as "infant, minor." In the context of Hebrews 5:13 the *nēpios* "is one who views spiritual things fr. [sic] the standpoint of a child." [4] So whether an infant who has not learned to talk or a minor who is incapable of using words with skill, the thought is clear that they are incapable of telling their experience to others. This is the curse of present-day Christianity.

But strong meat belongeth to them that are of full age [adults, full-grown men], even those who by reason of use have their senses exercised to discern both good and evil (v.14).

The readers should be not babes but adults in their Christian experience. It is such that can chew the strong meat of the word of God. **Full age** renders *teleiōn,* one who has achieved the goal or purpose of his being. That purpose being to be skilful in sharing the "word of righteousness." They are those who through use have their organs of perception "exercised to judge between good and evil." **Exercised** renders a form of *gumnazō* whence comes the word "gymnasium." Judgment between good and evil suggests a discernment as to what is proper food for the soul. Such discernment contributes to stability of character. It is this kind of Christian who is able to find and fill his place in God's service.

Thomas draws from this the principle of the Christian life "use or lose." [5] This is not to lose one's redemption but the ability to use one's spiritual "senses" through constant exercise. This the Hebrew Christians were failing to do. Their immaturity threatened their reason for being. Despite all that their High Priest had done to purify them for the Lord's work, they were failing in his purpose. It was this which led the author to issue another exhortation in chapter 6.

Notes

1. *Op. cit.,* p. 136; cf. Delitzsch, *op. cit.,* p. 263.
2. *Hebrews in the Greek New Testament,* Eerdmans, Grand Rapids, 1953, p. 107.
3. *Op. cit.,* p. 264.
4. *Op. cit.,* p. 539; cf. 1 Cor. 13:11.
5. *Op. cit.,* p. 69.

VI. The Challenge to Perseverance

Here is another case where chapter divisions may be confusing. For the author continued the thought which he was discussing in the previous chapter. He was concerned with the immaturity of his readers causing them to fall short of their destiny in God's world-mission. Having stated the fact he exhorted his readers to correct the situation.

1. The Third Exhortation (6:1-6)

This is one of the most difficult passages in Hebrews or the entire Bible to interpret. Its difficulties are exceeded only by the danger involved in a failure to discern its meaning. This danger will be dealt with in verses 4-6.

Therefore leaving the principles of the doctrine of Christ, let us go on unto perfection; not laying again the foundation of repentance from dead works, and of faith toward God, of the doctrine of baptisms, and of laying on of hands, and of resurrection from the dead, and of eternal judgment (vv. 1-2).

Does **therefore** or **wherefore** *(dio)* refer to the difficulty of interpretation and the dull readers? Or does it envelop the entire idea of spiritual immaturity? It would seem that the latter is true. So, "leaving the of-the-beginning-of-Christ-word." Robertson translates this, "Let us cease to speak of the first principles of Christ." [1] Westcott sees **the principles of the doctrine of Christ** as referring to the idea that Christ fulfilled the Old Testament messianic prophecies. [2] In either case the thought is to progress in Christian growth beyond the elementary things of the Christian revelation to a fuller growth and commitment in the Christian cause.

Let us go on unto perfection. He did not say, "Do not go back into Judaism" —or into a life of pagan sin—with the idea of losing their redemption. It is a call to go on from where they are to what God wills them to be, **unto perfection.** Actually "the perfection" or a particular perfection. **Perfection** means maturity, achieving a goal, or adulthood as opposed to infanthood.

The verb **let us go on** or "let us press on" renders a verb *pherō*, to bear. It is a volitive present subjunctive passive form. It speaks not of an action *by* the subject but of an action *to* the subject. So it may be rendered, "Let us be borne on." This is suggestive of 2:1. The author urges his readers to join him as they are borne along on the river of God's redemptive purpose. They should launch out into the river and be born on in God's world-mission, rather than to stand on the banks, their feet barely in the water, as they are flowed by. The exhortation is with respect to the danger of losing their opportunity in God's world-mission.

If they are to avoid this there are certain negative things to be done. They are summed up in **not laying again the foundation.** One can never construct a building if he spends all of his time on the foundation. Of what does this foundation consist?

Of repentance from dead works. Repentance is one of the great words of the gospel. It means a change of mind, heart, and attitude. It was the resounding note in the preaching of John the Baptist (Matt. 3:2), Jesus (Matt. 3:17), and the apostles (Acts 2:38).

But what did the author mean by **dead works** (cf. 9:14)? The New Testament often speaks of death in connection with sin. Men outside of Christ are dead in sin. Westcott sees this as referring to the Levitical system as incapable of producing spiritual life.[3] Actually it could be either. The readers could still be dwelling under the shadow of Judaism. Which would certainly deter them from their world-mission. Or it could mean their repentance from sin.

Schneider speaks of these **dead works** as "the doings of a man who does not confess God revealed in Christ [and] are without genuine and energizing power. His works cannot avail before God." He speaks of repentance as signifying "the complete break with all relations in thought and behaviour not subject to the lordship of the living God."[4]

In the light of 9:14 **dead works** probably has reference to the works done under the Levitical system in order to be purified from sin and to be fitted for the service of God. This also seems to fit the following phrase.

Of faith toward [*epi*] God. Rather than to trust in legal works one should trust in God. This is what the readers had done in order to be saved. They turned from faith in Levitical law toward God in faith for cleansing from sin.

Of the doctrine [teaching] of baptisms. The plural form "baptisms" causes one to look beyond Christian baptism to the Jewish practice of ceremonial cleansing through ablutions. The Greek word for Christian baptism is *baptisma,* referring not to the act but to the meaning in the act: death, burial, and resurrection. The word here is *baptismos,* the act itself. It is never used elsewhere in the New Testament for Christian baptism (cf. Mark 7:4; Heb. 6:2; 9:10). So this would seem to be one of the Jewish practices to which some readers still held.

Of laying on of hands. This custom was used variously: a sign of blessing (Matt. 19:13), of healing (Mark 7:32), the choice of the seven (Acts 6:6), the bestowal of the Holy Spirit (Acts 8:17; 19:6), ordination (1 Tim. 4:14), and of separation for a special service for God (Acts 13:3). Here this most likely had reference either to the reception of the Spirit or being set apart for special service. More likely for an entire congregation it refers to the Holy Spirit.

Of resurrection from the dead, and of eternal judgment. These were two basic teachings of the Christian faith. The mixture of Jewish and Christian elements suggests the immaturity of their faith. However, the exhortation **let us go on**

suggests that the readers were challenged to go beyond even the basic things of the Christian faith to launch out in a practical sharing of them with others. This would involve the world-mission. And the author proposed to lead them on, "if God permit" (v.3). Certainly such was/is in God's will.

Against this background the author expressed the heart of the matter. It is another warning not to fall short of their intended destiny in their Christian experience.

For it is impossible for those who were once enlightened, and have tasted of the heavenly gift, and were made partakers [partners, cf. 3:1] of the Holy Ghost [Spirit], and have tasted the good word of God, and the powers of the world to come, if they shall fall away, to renew them again unto repentance; seeing they crucify to themselves the Son of God afresh, and put him to an open shame (vv. 4–6).

It should be noted that **impossible** *(adunaton)* comes first in the sentence, and so is emphatic. In the sentence structure it is related to the infinitive "to renew again."

Some seek to tone down this expression by saying that it is impossible for men but not for God. But only God through the Holy Spirit produces repentance in the first place. The statement is *absolute*. **It is impossible . . . to renew them again unto repentance.** Whatever the author had in mind this statement does not allow for being toned down. Furthermore, this strong statement does not permit merely a *backsliding*. It involves a definite decision to turn away from someone or something.

Various interpretations have been given to verses 4–6. What was the condition of the readers and the purpose of the author? Some see the readers as Jews who were contemplating becoming Christians, but who had not yet done so. However, the writer sees this as an impossible position. The tone of the epistle, plus verses 4–5, seems to require its readers to be Christian people (cf. 3:1).

Others see the readers as having had a genuine Christian experience, but are in danger of losing it by renouncing Christ to return to Judaism. The ultimate position, of course, is that one can be saved and then lose his salvation through apostasy. If this be the meaning it runs counter to other clear teachings as to the security of the believer (cf. John 1:12; 3:16; 5:24; 10:28–29; Rom. 8:16–17, 29–39; Gal. 4:4–7; Eph. 1:13–14; 2:8–10; Col. 3:3).

One will strive in vain to show that Judas, for instance, was ever a true believer in Jesus. The sin against the Holy Spirit, to which some allude in this connection, is possible only to those who have never received Jesus as Saviour. Galatians 5:4 does not teach that one in grace can fall from grace. Its entire context speaks of one who chooses the *law* and not the *grace* way of salvation.

There are those who seek to get around this dilemma by saying that a genuine faith will be a persevering faith. This is true. But the author assumed a true faith. Others suggest that the author was using a hypothetical case which could not really happen. But he was too skilled a sermonizer to do this. What he referred to can happen, and was in danger of happening to his readers. Why use a hypothetical case at all? For either one can apostatize or one cannot. And if it be admitted that one can have salvation and lose it, this passage clearly says that he can never be saved again.

It is evident from this volume thus far that the writer understands the New Testament to teach that, when one receives Christ by grace through faith, his redemption is complete and final. He has *everlasting* life (cf. John 5:24). And everlasting means everlasting, and in no sense conditional or temporary, if language means anything. It did not depend upon man's work in the beginning. Its permanence does not depend upon man. It is by grace through faith, a gift of God appropriated by man through faith. Ephesians 2:8–9 says that it is "not out of [source] yourselves . . . not out of works." It is "of God the gift." "Are ye saved" or "have been saved" (perfect) in verse 8 means a completed work. And the author of Hebrews assumed that his readers had had that experience.

However, if one agrees that salvation is threefold: regeneration (instantaneous), sanctification (an instantaneous state with continuing development in it), and glorification (ultimate state of the redeemed), the problem would appear to be lessened, perhaps solved altogether. Thus it would appear that the author was not speaking of losing one's regeneration, but of the danger involved in a state of arrested development in Christian growth by which his readers were in peril of falling short of their ultimate purpose in Christian service in God's world-mission. If this be a true position, then the warning is related to what happens in the state of sanctification with the final result reflected in glorification. In this light, therefore, a close examination of the passage is in order.

Recall the interpretation of 3:12. Israel as a people redeemed from Egyptian bondage failed to achieve her destiny in Canaan as a priest-nation. This was due to her rebellion against God. It seems that the author faced a similar situation involving these Hebrew Christians. It should be kept in mind also that the author used the allegorical method of interpretation as he applied events connected with the Exodus epic to his readers and their problem. He was saying that they should not let the same thing happen to them.

The spiritual experiences listed in verses 4–5 should be compared with those of Israel at Kadesh-barnea which led up to the rebellion of Israel. When the twelve spies returned from Canaan they brought back a glowing report of the land of Canaan. The Israelities were *enlightened* as to its condition (Num. 13:26–27; 14:7). They brought back samples of the fruit of the land (Num. 13:26–27). They, in a sense, tasted of its wonders. They were aware of their covenant as a priest-nation (Ex. 19:5–6). They were to be God's *partners* in a world-mission. They were exhorted as to God's promise to give them that land and that he would enable them to conquer it (Num. 13:2; 14:8–9). They *tasted* of the good (sure) word of God, and his power to give them victory in the land they were about to inherit. And then with all of this experience, still they rebelled against God. They refused to enter the land from which they were to fill their role as a priest-nation.

Now apply these to the Hebrew Christians. They had been **once enlightened.**

Once renders *hapax,* once-for-all. They had experienced regeneration and sanctification. As God's redeemed people they had been set apart for his service. They had **tasted of the heavenly gift.** They knew the experience of being a people of God with the assurance of the joys of heaven. They **were made partakers** [partners, cf. 3:1] **of the Holy Ghost** [Spirit] in a mission for God in propagating the gospel (cf. Acts 1:8). They had **tasted the good word of God, and the powers of the world to come** or "the powers of the about-to-be age." They had Christ's assurance of his presence and power in achieving their purpose to disciple all nations (Matt. 28:18–20). Whether these be exact parallels with Israel or not, they speak of definite spiritual experiences which should prompt them to faithfulness.

And yet **if they shall fall away.** The verb is a participle *parapesontas* from *parapiptō,* to fall alongside. It is used only here in the New Testament. It should be noted that the verb forms "enlightened," "tasted," "made," and "fall away" are all aorist tenses, expressing actions which happened one time. This is significant when compared with the present tenses of "renew," "crucify," and "put."

But how may one regard **shall fall away?** It is used in the papyri for breaking a contract. Moulton and Milligan cite an example: "if the terms of it (sc. a contract) should be broken or it in any other way be rendered invalid." this work comments, "Supports the sinister meaning in Hebrews 6:6" [5] Moffatt says, "*Parapiptein*. . . corresponds to *apostēnai* (3:12), and indeed both verbs are used in the LXX to translate the same term, " [6] that term meaning "deed" in its evil aspect. But he proceeds to relate both to *apostasy* in the popular sense of that word.

However, following the use of *apostēnai* as revealed in the use of its derivatives in the papyri, *parapiptō* may be seen in the same sense as rebellion against the living God. So the author again as in 3:12 saw the possibility that his readers would rebel against God as he sought to lead them into the fulfilment of their world-mission. This would mean that they had broken their covenant or *contract* with God.

Now, said he, if this should happen what would be the result? It would be **impossible . . . to renew them again unto repentance,** a change of mind, attitude, and heart. What, in the experience at Kadesh-barnea, may correspond to this?

Because of Israel's rebellion, God finally decreed that while "all the earth shall be filled with the glory of the Lord" (Num. 14:21), none of that generation of Israelites above nineteen years of age, save Caleb and Joshua, would enter the land of Canaan (Num. 14:23 ff.). Their covenant was conditional. They had not kept the **if** so Jehovah was not bound by the "then" (cf. Ex. 19:5–6). Thus he said, "As ye have spoken in mine ears [rebelling against their covenant], so will I do to you [he would not use them under the covenant]: Your carcases shall fall in the wilderness; and all that were numbered of you, according to your whole number, from twenty-years old and upward, which have murmured against me" (Num. 14:28 f.). They were not sent back into the unredeemed state of bondage in Egypt. They lost their opportunity as a generation and died in the wilderness.

God's work would go on, but they would be flowed by. He would use another generation for his priest-nation.

A given generation of God's people may *delay* his purpose, but they will not defeat it. If he cannot use one people he will use another. God's redemptive purpose never changes. But he changes his method and instruments according to his will and the will of his people.

Now drop down to Numbers 14:40. Apparently the leaders of the tribes held a consultation about the matter. They feared the Canaanites, but they feared their gruesome fate more. Better to die trying to enter Canaan than to live and die in the desert land.

"And they rose up early in the morning, and got them up into the top of the mountain, saying, Lo, we be here, and will go up unto the place which the Lord hath promised: for we have sinned."

They wanted to *repent,* to change their minds, hearts, and attitudes. But Moses told them that this was *impossible* (Num. 14:41 f.). God had decreed, and it could not be changed. Certainly this event corresponds to the words in Hebrews 6. **It is impossible . . . to renew them again unto repentance** (cf. 12:16 f.).

A given group of God's people, a church, or an individual Christian may so rebel against God's world-mission as to lose the opportunity of being used in it. A given church through lack of evangelism sees that it is slowly dying. So it decides that for self-preservation it will change its ways, only to find that it has reached the point of no return. One should not trifle with his covenant relation to God with respect to his world-mission.

Why could not these Hebrew Christians repent if they made this fatal choice? Because **they crucify to themselves the Son of God afresh, and put him to an open shame** (v.6).

The word **afresh** should not be in the text. The verb does read *anastauroō, ana,* again, prefixed to the verb "to crucify." But this was an old Greek verb meaning simply to crucify. Those who see *apostasy* in this passage understand this to mean that for such to be saved again Christ would have to die on a cross again. This, of course, will not be. But, as seen above, this idea is not allowed in this verb.

The meaning seems to be that those who rebel against God's redemptive purpose in his world-mission join with those who crucified Jesus in open disgrace. He was crucified as a criminal, his naked body being made a spectacle of shame. They crucified Christ in rebellion against God. While God overruled it to perform his redemptive purpose through it, that was not in the purpose of the rebels. They sought to destroy Jesus, to negate God's purpose of the ages.

That is exactly what Christians do when they refuse to be involved in God's program of evangelism and missions. The end result insofar as their lives are concerned, as well as lost souls to whom they do not witness, is to negate God's redemptive purpose. Thus they join with the crucifiers. God's purpose goes on in another place, another time. But, for the rebels, their opportunity is lost forever.

Mention was made of the tenses of the verbs in verses 4–6. Beginning with "enlightened" and running through "fall away" the tense is an aorist of point action. In a sense this is the historical tense. If at any time these things happen to one, then the impossibility abides. At a given point in time one may rebel against God's purpose. Thereafter, a change of attitude and action is impossible.

To renew, crucify, and **put to shame** are present tenses. This is the tense of repeated action in the present. It may also express action *from time to time.* And this meaning fits here. As often as one, having experienced the things mentioned in verses 4–5, *rebels at a given time,* then from time to time (when each one does this) he joins with those who crucified and shamed Jesus and, therefore, from time to time cannot be renewed unto repentance. This happened to Israel at Kadesh-barnea. It was in danger of happening to these Hebrew Christians. It can happen to God's people anywhere, anytime they rebel against God's world-mission!

2. The Example from Nature (6:7–8)

Having stated his case the author illustrated it from nature. It reminds one of the parable of the sower or soils (cf. Matt. 13:3 ff.). The same seed fell on different soils, but with different results. The difference was in neither the sower nor the seed, but in the soils. Likewise, the same good tidings of God's redemptive purpose (cf. 4:2 ff.) fell on all of Israel but with different results. This seems to be the point in these verses.

For the earth which drinketh in the rain that cometh oft upon it, and bringeth forth herbs meet for them by whom it is dressed, receiveth blessing from God (v.7).

The earth suggests Israel who had received God's blessings (cf. Isa. 5; Matt. 21:33–46). That which produces **herbs** fit for the one who tills the soil is blessed of God. Implied here is that God himself is both tiller and the one blessing. In one sense Moses was the tiller. But he acted for God. He had blessed his people that they might be a blessing (cf. Gen. 12:2). Of this generation first out of Egypt, Caleb and Joshua alone had proved faithful to the covenant.

But that which beareth thorns and briers is rejected, and is nigh unto cursing; whose end is to be burned (v.8).

In Matthew 7:16 the same words are translated "thorns and thistles." These are good for nothing and are a waste on the land. They use the rain and soil to produce nothing of value. **Rejected** renders a word which in 1 Corinthians 9:27 is rendered "castaway." Such land is "nigh unto a curse." This is suggestive of Numbers 14:12 ff. God threatened to "disinherit" (rejected) Israel, "smite" her with a pestilence, and destroy her (cf. Num. 14:15). But for Moses' intercession all these things would have befallen the rebellious nation.

Instead she was doomed to a fruitless life of lost opportunity. This also suggests the words **whose end is to be burned.** The products of the land, thorns and briers, were burned, not the land itself. This reminds one of 1 Corinthians 3:13–15. There Paul spoke of Christians who would be saved, but whose useless works would be burned up. Such works are good only "for burning" (v.8).

These Hebrew Christians had received God's blessings. But they were bearing only **thorns and briers.** They also were "nigh unto a curse," and continuing their present rebellious conduct would see their useless works good only "for burning." Not the Christians but their works would perish.

3. The Encouragement to Faithfulness (6:9–12)

After this terrible warning the author turned to loving his readers. In so doing he sought to challenge them to change their attitude while opportunity remained to do so.

But, beloved, we are persuaded better things of you, the things that accompany salvation, though we thus speak (v.9).

His explanatory words "though we are speaking thus" do not mean that he pulled his punches. He was letting them know the reason for his harsh words. They were the preventive chastisement of one who loved them. He was *fully persuaded* (perfect tense of completeness) that they would do better than their Israelite forebears. He was certain that they would do "the better things . . . which accompany salvation." Literally, "holding salvation." This does not mean holding on to their redemption.

Westcott notes two possible meanings: things which issue into salvation, or things which issue from salvation.[7] Good works do not produce salvation. But they should result from it (cf. Eph. 2:8–10). In the light of the overall context the latter seems to be the meaning here. In their state of regeneration and sanctification they should produce works which are commensurate with it. In the context of the epistle's purpose this suggests being used in God's world-mission.

For God is not unrighteous [unjust] to forget your work and labour of love, which ye have shewed toward his name, in that ye have ministered to the saints, and do minister (v.10).

Labour is not in the best texts. So "your work and love" which they demonstrated toward God's name. **Ministered . . . do minister** renders an aorist and a present tense respectively, "ministered and keep on ministering." These things had been and were being done to their fellow Christians. But even these things were far short of what they should do. They should also witness to the lost. It was a case of this they should do and not to leave the other undone (cf. Matt. 23:23). Robertson comments that "even God cannot remember what they did not do."[8]

A church should do more than minister to its own. It should be reaching out to win the mass of paganism which surrounds it.

And we desire that every one of you do shew the same diligence to the full assurance of hope unto the end (v.11). The author was not fully satisfied with the conduct of his readers (cf. 5:11–14). Even though they were doing some good things they were falling short of their potential. So he expressed the desire that each of them would demonstrate the same diligence "unto the fulness of hope until the end." This does not mean to *hold out* in faith until the end of life. The word **end** *(telous)* suggests a goal. They should show the same zeal in other matters as in their love for one another. They should be concerned about others, namely, those outside the Christian fellowship. Their God-given goal was primarily to be a holy nation of priests to a lost world, to bring it to receive Christ and to worship and serve God.

That ye be not slothful, but followers of them who through faith and patience inherit the promises (v.12).

Slothful renders *nōthroi* (cf. 5:11, "dull"). They are *stupid* students (Plato). And their ears and hearts are deadened to their world-mission. The word **that** *(hina)* relates this verse to the *goal* expressed in verse 11. Their intellectual immaturity was in danger of diverting them from their life purpose.

So the author challenged them to be **followers** (*mimētai,* imitators) of those who had persevered in faith and patience to **inherit the promises. Patience** *(makrothumias)* expresses the trial of unsatisfied desire. As Christians they wanted to do God's will. But they had been unwilling to pay the price in doing it. Persecution, immaturity, and lack of dedication were the trials.

Inherit the promises suggests the promises made to Abraham and his seed (cf. vv. 13 f.). These involved entering into their *rest* and serving therein. As they were blessed they should be a blessing. **Them** evidently points forward to the heroes of faith which the author will discuss at length in chapter 11. The Hebrew Christians were heirs of the fruit of faith and patience of those who preceded them. They were not a generation in isolation, but were one segment in the fellowship of God's redemptive purpose through the ages. They are to use this fruit so as to share it with their contemporaries and pass it on to succeeding generations.

4. The Promise of God (6:13–18)

Here the author definitely explained the *promises* as that made to Abraham. The plural of *promises* probably refers to the one major promise (cf. Gen. 12:1–3) which was repeated on several occasions. The reference here is to the reavowal of the promise made to Abraham after his near-sacrifice of Isaac (cf. Gen. 22:16–18).

For when God made promise to Abraham, because he could swear by no greater, he sware by himself, saying, Surely blessing I will bless thee, and multiplying I will multiply thee (vv. 13–14).

No greater trial of faith can be imagined than that when God told Abraham to sacrifice his son through whom God's promise was to run (cf. 11:17 ff.). But when he proved faithful, God swore by himself, the highest possible oath, that he would produce a nation through whom the whole world would receive the spiritual blessing. Thus it was that when Abraham stood the test of his unsatisfied desire (patience, cf. v.12), he obtained the assurance that God would fulfil his promise.

Actually the word for **patience** *(makrothumos)* means *long spirit.* The patriarch's spirit reached beyond the trial of the moment to see the fulfilment of the promise in God's own time and way.

The readers of this epistle were hung up on the trial of the moment. They needed to look beyond the moment to see God's power to enable them to be true to their world-mission. As one said, they needed to see what the centuries said against the hours. As Christians see the tremendous challenge of world missions they should cease seeing God through their trials and see their trials through God.

For men verily swear by the greater: and an oath for confirmation is to them an end of all strife (v.16).

Even at the human level men take an oath by the greater authority. And such a guarantee is among them the end of all discussion, **strife**, or talking back. If this be true, then it should be infinitely so between men and God. God took an oath to demonstrate the "immutability of his counsel," or the unchangeable nature of his will (v.17). Under Hebrew law two witnesses were necessary to establish a matter (v.18). God's two witnesses were his *promise* and his *oath.* God cannot lie. So these two witnesses are the Christian's abiding assurance in the hope or goal which is before him. This hope is that of securing the promise. Therefore, by God's promise and oath they should seize their opportunity, knowing that he who promised and swore to perform can enable them to fulfil their destiny.

5. The Anchor of Assurance (6:19–20)

The hope of receiving the full promise made by God to Abraham, and in which these Hebrew Christians shared, is assured by Jesus, the High Priest. It is in him that his people must trust as they carry forward his redemptive purpose.

Which hope we have as an anchor of the soul, both sure and stedfast, and which entereth into that within the veil; whither the forerunner is for us entered, even Jesus, made an high priest for ever after the order of Melchisedec (vv. 19–20).

The figure of an **anchor** suggests safety and stability (cf. Acts 27:29). The words **sure and stedfast** (*bebaian,* guaranteed) suggest that it is strong and will not slip and also that it is guaranteed and trustworthy. This anchor has come into "the inner part of the veil" or the Holy of Holies into God's presence.

Ironside relates an interesting custom in ancient seafaring.[9] Sometimes sandbars across the entrance to a port made it impossible for large vessels to enter the port at low tide. So a sailor (forerunner) in a small boat would take the anchor across the sandbar and let it down in the harbor. Thus the ship was held steady and safe. When the tide rose it would enter the harbor.

Thomas tells a similar story although he admits that he had not had opportunity to verify its accuracy. But the two varying accounts throw light on these verses.

Jesus, the **forerunner** (*prodromos,* spy or scout) has entered into the harbor, the heavenly Holy of Holies (9:12). There he holds intercession for his people still on earth (7:25). His presence there is their assurance that the promise will be kept. So he is the *prodromos* taking the anchor within the veil, the harbor. His people on earth, like a cargo-ladened ship, must stay in the open sea for a while. They may experience the fury of wind and waves. But they are held stedfast and sure as they go on bearing the precious cargo of God's redemptive world-mission. In due time God's tide will rise and they will enter into the heavenly harbor bringing a cargo of saved souls with them.

This enduring High-priestly work of Jesus shows him to be after the order of Melchisedec. The figure in verses 19–20 completes the picture of Jesus as "a priest for ever after the order of Melchisedec" (5:6). He is the High Priest making the sacrifice, which sacrifice is himself. He has taken the evidence of the atonement within the veil. And there he holds intercession for his own. It is this assurance which should lead his people in every generation to persevere in their God-given world-mission.

Notes

1. *Op. cit.*, p. 373.
2. *Op. cit.*, p. 144.
3. *Op. cit.*, p. 146.
4. *Op. cit.*, p. 49; cf. Archer, *op. cit.*, p. 39.
5. *Op. cit.*, pp. 488 f.
6. *Op. cit.*, p. 79.
7. *Op. cit.*, p. 156.
8. *Op. cit.*, p. 377.
9. *Hebrews and Titus*, Loizeaux, New York, 1950, p. 84; cf. Thomas, *Op. cit.*, footnote, p. 79.

VII. The Superior Priesthood

At this point the author of Hebrews had reached a climax in drawing his primary lesson from the Exodus epic. He had shown clearly what would happen to his readers if they made the same mistake as Israel in rebelling against their covenant as a priest-nation. Throughout the preceding chapters he had made reference to various elements in the Levitical system. So in chapters 7–10 he fortified his warning and exhortation by showing the superiority of the Christian covenant over the Mosaic covenant. Throughout this section one may see the veiled suggestion that rebellion against the new covenant will bring more serious consequences even than that under the old covenant. The matter dealt with in this chapter was that of Jesus' superior High-priesthood.

1. The Office and Nature of Melchisedec (7:1-3)

Previous mention had been made of Jesus being a priest after the order of Melchisedec (cf. 5:10; 6:20). Now the author proceeded to explain what he meant by this idea.

For this Melchisedec, king of Salem, priest of the most high God, who met Abraham returning from the slaughter of the kings, and blessed him (v.1).

For this the Melchisedec. This points to the one already mentioned. Who was this Melchisedec? He is mentioned only twice in the Old Testament (cf. Gen. 14:18–20; Psalm 110). It is evident, therefore, that he preceded Moses and the Levitical priesthood. His relation to Abraham also suggests that the readers of the epistle are related to the promise of God made to this patriarch. And in a very real sense their new covenant goes back to him (see chap. 8).

Melchisedec was **king of Salem.** The Hebrew word for **king,** *melek,* may be seen in **Melchisedec** (cf. v.2). Where was **Salem?** Josephus (*Antiquities* 1. 10, 2) refers it to Jerusalem. Westcott notes that in the time of Jerome, Salem was identified as the one near Scythopolis, where the remains of Melchisedec's palace were shown. The writer is inclined to agree with Josephus. However, the exact meaning of **Salem** (peace) is not too important to the author's purpose. The more important thing is that he was a **king.** He was a king-priest, which is important in his comparison with Jesus who was/is Prophet, Priest, and King.

Furthermore, Melchisedec was a **priest of the most high God.** Or "of God-Most High." The Hebrew is *El-elyon.* This was one of the titles applied to God by the Hebrews as well as by other ancient peoples to their god.

Some interpreters see him as a priest of Baal. However, others think it unlikely that the worship of Baal, the god of Phoenicia, had penetrated this far south into Palestine by the time of Abraham. Westcott notes, "It is to be remarked that there are elsewhere traces of a primitive (monotheistic) worship of El in Phoenicia side by side with that of Baal, the centre of Phoenician polytheism." [1] It should be noted that in Genesis 14:22, Abraham, a worshiper of Jehovah, referred to him as "the most high God [*El-elyon*], the possessor of heaven and earth" (cf. v.19). There is no real reason to doubt that Melchisedec was a priest of the one true God. However, even if some insist otherwise, it does not really affect the author's figure. For Jesus was not an exact replica of Melchisedec, but was after his *order* (cf. v.3).

Melchisedec's one appearance in the Old Testament *history* was when he went out to bless Abraham when he returned from a military expedition to rescue Lot (cf. Gen. 14:1 ff.).

To whom also Abraham gave a tenth part of all [the spoils of war]; **first being by interpretation King of righteousness, and after that also King of Salem, which is, King of peace** (v.2).

This is the first biblical mention of the tithe. That Abraham gave tithes to Melchisedec shows that he regarded him as a priest of God. **King of righteousness** is a translation of **Melchisedec. Salem** means "peace."

Without father, without mother, without descent, having neither beginning of days, nor end of life; but made like unto the Son of God; abideth a priest continually (v.3).

Without descent renders a word found nowhere else *(agenealogētos),* probably coined by the author, meaning "without genealogy." One should not press the description of Melchisedec beyond the simple meaning of the text. It simply means that in the biblical account there is no mention of his parents, genealogy, birth, or death. There is no record at the beginning or end of his priesthood. He stands alone in the record. He simply appears, and that is all.

The words **made like** mean that he was a copy of what the Son of God is. So he was made like unto the Son of God, not the Son like him. The author used **the Son of the God,** definitely referring to Jesus Christ. He also stands alone in his being with no other like him.

Of course, Jesus did have an earthly mother and a divine Father. The Gospels of Matthew and Luke give his genealogy and birth. All four Gospels relate his death, but also his continuing life. The point, however, is that as Melchisedec stands alone in his priesthood, Jesus is unique in his. There is no historical record of his appointment to such, and it continues for ever.

2. The Greatness of Melchisedec (7:4–10)

Now consider how great this man was, unto whom even the patriarch Abraham gave the tenth of his spoils (v.4).

Abraham was the father of the Hebrew people. Yet he recognized the right of Melchisedec to receive tithes from him. This showed the patriarch's recognition of his dignity and position above him. This would be a compelling argument to the Hebrew Christians.

The Levitical priests received tithes of the Hebrew people even though they are descendants of Abraham (v.5).

But he whose descent [genealogy] is not counted from them received tithes of Abraham, and blessed him that had the promises (v.6).

This repeats the thought in verse 4, and adds the idea of Melchisedec's blessing Abraham. Here again is the idea of his superiority over Abraham. For without question the greater blesses the lesser (v.7). Note the reference to the *promise* in verse 6. Compare v.21.

Furthermore, the Levites who die receive tithes of Abraham's descendants. But Melchisedec **of whom it is witnessed that he liveth** [present tense, keeps on living] received tithes from their father (v.8). This does not mean that Melchisedec never died. The author is drawing a comparison from the Genesis record which does not record his death. One should not press the details but should grasp the lesson taught by the author. He is using the Alexandrian method of interpretation commonly found in Philo, the Jewish-Alexandrian philosopher.

And as I may say, Levi also, who receiveth tithes, paid tithes in Abraham. For he was yet in the loins of his father [Abraham], when Melchisedec met him (vv. 9–10).

As I may say means "so to say." The author said that, in effect, Levi paid tithes to Melchisedec in the person of his forefather Abraham. This proves the superiority of Melchisedec's office over that of Levi, the father of the priestly tribe in Israel.

Running throughout this argument is the superiority of Christ's priesthood over that of the Levites. For he is a priest after the order of Melchisedec.

3. The Imperfection of the Levitical Priesthood (7:11–21)

In these verses the author showed why a greater priesthood was necessary. The very imperfection of the Levitical order pointed toward a perfect one.

If therefore perfection were by the Levitical priesthood, (for under it the people received the law,) what further need was there that another priest should rise after the order of Melchisedec, and not be called after the order of Aaron? (v.11).

Perfection *(teleiōsis)* does not refer to quality but function. The Levitical priesthood functioned under the Mosaic law. The repetition of its ministry of sacrifice showed that it did not bring man into a right relation to God. Had it done so there would not have been a need for **another** priestly order to be given. **Another** renders *heteros,* another of a different kind, perfect as opposed to the imperfection of the Levitical order. Otherwise, the priesthood of Christ would have been in the order of Aaron, the first Israelite high priest, and not in that of Melchisedec.

For the priesthood being changed, there is made of necessity a change also

of the law (v.12).

The words **changed** and "change" render a word meaning to set aside or transfer. The Levitical order was set aside as the office was transferred to another. The priesthood of law was changed to one of grace.

For he of whom these things are spoken pertaineth to another [*heteras*] tribe, of which no man gave attendance at the altar. For it is evident that our Lord sprang out of Juda; of which tribe Moses spake nothing concerning priesthood (vv. 13–14).

The author was coming to the heart of his argument. He was speaking of the priesthood of Jesus who came out of **another,** other than the priestly tribe of Levi. He was out of the tribe of Judah, no member of which ever ministered before the altar in the tabernacle. The perfect tense of **gave attendance** expresses finality or completeness. Moses never at any time "spake" (aorist tense) of the tribe in terms of priesthood.

And it is yet far more evident: for that after the similitude of Melchisedec there ariseth another [*heteros*, another of a different kind than Aaron] priest (v.15).

Far more renders a word meaning to overflow. The evidence stated in verse 14 is even more clearly shown in Jesus being a priest after the likeness of Melchisedec.

Who is made, not after the law of a carnal commandment, but after the power of an endless life (v.16).

Made renders *ginomai,* to become. Those who before were not priests became such by a carnal commandment. The Levitical priesthood was brought into being by Moses, and thereafter those priests were born into the office. But Jesus *was* such by the power of an indissoluble life. His High-priesthood was co-existent with his sonship and had no end. To prove his argument the author cited again Psalm 110:4 (v.17).

The Levitical priesthood was *set aside* or made void because of its weakness and its unprofitable or useless nature (v.18; cf. v.11). The ministry under "the law made nothing perfect" or failed to effect a right relation to God (v.19). **But the bringing in of a better hope did; by which we draw nigh unto God** (v.19). **Bringing in** was used by Josephus (*Ant. XI.* 6,2) for bringing in a new wife to replace the one who had been cast aside. Here the thought is that a better priesthood with a better hope was brought in to replace that which was repudiated because it could not bring men to God. To **draw nigh** to God suggests those who had been purified and made fit instruments for his use. The readers of this epistle were such (cf. 4:16).

And inasmuch as not without an oath he was made priest: (For those priests were made without an oath; but this with an oath by him that said unto him, The Lord sware and will not repent [change mind, heart, or attitude], Thou art a priest for ever after the order of Melchisedec) (vv. 20–21).

Here the author completed the thought expressed in 6:13–18. God's covenant with Abraham was guaranteed by his *promise* and *oath* (cf. 7:6,20 f.). This the author also related to Jesus' abiding priesthood which he proceeded to discuss in verses 22–28.

4. The Unchangeable Priesthood (7:22–24)

Contrary to the Levitical priesthood, that of Jesus is unchangeable. He abides a priest forever.

By so much was Jesus made a surety of a better testament (v.22).

By so much refers to God's oath. It was thus that Jesus became a **surety of a better testament** or "covenant" *(diathekē)*. This is the word used for the Old and New *Testaments*. The thought here is the new covenant of grace as over against the old one of law under Moses.

Surety *(egguos)* was used of a pledge or guarantee. So Jesus in his priesthood guarantees the grace covenant. Usually a guarantee has reference to some future performance. But Jesus pledges the efficacy of his finished saving work, a past performance. He is not a guarantee for man to God, but of God's covenant with man.

And they truly were many priests, because they were not suffered to continue by reason of death: but this man, because he continueth ever, hath an unchangeable priesthood (vv. 23–24).

The Levitical priests died, and new ones took their places (cf. Ex. 40:15, "throughout their generation"). But it is through Jesus' death and resurrection that he is able to be a continuing priest whose office is inviolate. No one will ever replace him **ever** or "unto the age."

Here then is another evidence of the superiority of Jesus' priesthood over that of the Levitical order. It corresponds to the order of Melchisedec. But there remained one further proof.

5. The Perfect Sacrifice (7:25–28)

Jesus is not only the perfect priest; he is also the perfect sacrifice. *Perfect* in this sense means that he avails to bring believers into a right relation with God.

Wherefore he is able also to save them to the uttermost that come unto God by him, seeing he ever liveth to make intercession for them (v.25).

Wherefore refers back to Jesus' unchanging priesthood. For this reason he is powerful *to save to the uttermost.* **The uttermost** does not mean *in perpetuum* or eternally as in the Vulgate. The idea is present but only by implication. The phrase *eis to panteles* means completely or utterly. This is suggestive of regeneration, sanctification, and glorification. He is able to save not only the soul but the Christian life—the ultimate end being glorification in heaven. This would be a needed promise to these Hebrew Christians.

But notice that this promise is made only to those who **come unto God**. Not only their faith in regeneration but faithful obedience in the state of sanctification. Rebellion against God's world-mission would not cancel regeneration. But it would mean loss of opportunity in the state of sanctification—and a loss of glory and reward in heaven.

Of interest is the fact that "came unto" is a middle voice. God does not force men to come to him. They must do it within themselves, of their own will. Neither does he force his people to serve him in the world-mission. They are free to choose, but are held responsible for their choice.

Jesus is able to save utterly because he is always living **to make intercession** for those who trust in him. This is the thought expressed in 1 John 2:1. "And if any man sin, we have an advocate with the Father, Jesus Christ the righteous." "Advocate" renders *parakletos,* one called alongside. See "Comforter" in John 14:16 of the Holy Spirit. The Holy Spirit is God's Advocate before men's hearts. Jesus the High Priest is the believer's Advocate before the Father.

This word was used of a lawyer called to stand beside one in court, especially the lawyer for the defence. Thus Jesus pleads for forgiveness when believers sin. This would apply when they are tempted to sin against their covenant relation. Moses interceded for Israel at Kadesh-barnea that she would not be destroyed or disinherited (cf. Num. 14:13 ff.). But because she had rebelled she did lose her opportunity as a generation. The Hebrew Christians had not yet rebelled but were in danger of doing so. Jesus is pleading before God that they shall have strength not to take this fatal step.

For such an high priest became us, who is holy, harmless, undefiled, separate from sinners, and made higher than the heavens (v.26).

A High Priest after the order of Melchisedec fitted the needs of sinners such as the readers then and now. He is absolute in power (v.25) and eternal in being (v.24). *He is able* and *He ever liveth.*

The characteristics of this High Priest are set forth. **Holy** (*hosios,* saintly) is different from *hagios,* dedicated, set apart to God's service. It means that Jesus partakes of the very nature of God. **Harmless** *(akakos)* means guileless, innocent, or without evil (cf. 4:15). He remained so despite the fact that he lived in an evil world. **Undefiled** *(amiantos)* expresses something of the same idea, except that it stresses the fact that no impurity ever affected his priestly function. He was ethically clean. These three things express both Jesus' deity and humanity.

The remaining two ideas relate to his exaltation in heaven after his resurrection. He is **separate** or "separated from sinners." The perfect tense stresses the completeness of his removal out of the visible order as he is **made higher than the heavens** or has entered into the very presence of God. His experience on earth makes him the perfect High Priest sympathetic with his people's needs (cf 5:2,8 f.). And his presence with the Father enables him to continue his high priestly intercession.

Who needeth not daily, as those high priests, to offer up sacrifice, first for their own sins, and then for the people's: for this he did once, when he offered up himself (v.27).

The high priests under the old order offered repeated sacrifices, for themselves and then for the people. But Christ made a "once-for-all" *(ephapax)* sacrifice when he sacrificed himself. He was both High Priest and Sacrifice.

A problem arises with respect to the **daily** sacrifice on the part of the high priest. He made the sacrifice on the annual Day of Atonement. Some see **daily** *(kath' hēmeran)* to mean on each Day of Atonement; others that the high priest daily felt the necessity of such a sacrifice. Perhaps a better sense is that the priests daily made sacrifices in which at times the high priest participated. The priests acted for the high priest. So in that sense he did act daily. And the annual sacrifice on the Day of Atonement in a sense climaxed all the daily sacrifices.

However one may regard this, the author's primary thought was that by contrast Jesus, the superior High Priest, made only a once-for-all sacrifice in himself.

The daily sacrifices actually complemented the annual sacrifice. The annual sacrifice was as an atonement for the sins of the previous year. The daily sacrifices were intended to purify sinners from their day-to-day sins. Thus they were purified for God's service. In his one sacrifice Jesus accomplished both results. He atoned for *sin,* and he cleanses from *sins,* so that the Hebrew Christians were fit instruments for God's service.

For the law maketh men high priests which have infirmity; but the word of the oath, which was since the law, maketh the [a, no definite article] Son, who is consecrated for evermore (v.28).

The Levitical high priesthood was incomplete in every sense. The high priest was a servant before God's altar. Jesus was one bearing the relation of Son (cf. 1:2; 3:6) who ministered before his own altar.

He is "unto the age having been perfected" or completely fitted to fill the role of the eternal High Priest. As the Divine-Human Son of God he perfectly represents both God and man. He is divinely appointed with an oath. He is sympathetic with sinners. He made the once-for-all sacrifice in himself. And he ever lives to hold intercession for his people.

The Hebrew Christians were the beneficiaries of Jesus' superior high priestly ministry. They were in a new covenant with him, partners with him and the Holy Spirit (cf. 3:1; 6:4), in God's world-mission. And as Jesus is superior to the high priest under the old covenant, so his people bear a greater obligation to declare his gospel to a lost world. There is no need for another sacrifice, neither will there be one. The work is finished (cf. John 19:30). God but waits on his people to declare it.

Note

1. *Op. cit.,* p. 173.

VIII. The New Covenant

The burden of Hebrews 7–10 is a contrast between the ministry under the old and new covenants. In chapter 7 the central thought was the High-priesthood under each covenant. Chapter 8 has to do with the covenants themselves. It shows how and why the old covenant was replaced by the new.

1. The Summary Statement (8:1–2)

Actually this idea runs through verse 5. However, these verses seem to deal with, first, a summary statement, and, second, a brief description of the priestly ministry under the old covenant and its comparison with the ministry of the High Priest under the new covenant.

Now of the things which we have spoken this is the sum: We have such an high priest, who is set on the right hand of the throne of the Majesty in the heavens; a ministry of the sanctuary, and of the true tabernacle, which the Lord pitched, and not man (vv. 1–2).

The Greek text begins with the word *kephalaion* or **sum.** This word comes from *kephalē*, head. Some interpreters see this as **sum** or "summary." The idea is that of adding up a column of figures from below and placing the sum of them at the head of the column. Others see it as "chief point" or the heart of the matter. Actually the end result fits either idea. But the latter idea seems to be the better. The author was giving the main thought of what he had said in chapter 7 as introductory to chapter 8.

Such an high priest suggests specifically 7:26–28. But that which follows broadens the picture to include the joint-ministry of Jesus as both *Priest* and *King.* Having finished his sacrifice once-for-all he is seated on the heavenly throne of power and glory.

Marcus Dods extends *such an high priest* to include not only that which preceded but also that which followed.[1] Jesus is such an High Priest who **sat down** on his heavenly throne to continue his ministry in his unchangeable priesthood (cf. 7:25). This ministry is treated in the following chapters.

The first point that the author made is with regard to the better sanctuary in which Jesus ministers as High Priest. Actually, "of the Holy Places a minister." Note the plural. It includes both the Holy Place where the sacrifice was made and the Holy of Holies into which the blood of the sacrifice was taken (cf.

9:12). This figure was drawn from the tabernacle in the wilderness, the one in which Aaron served as high priest. It was actually a large tent (*skēnē;* cf. Matt. 17:4; John 1:14; 2 Cor. 5:1). It was made by men and was pitched and taken down by men as Israel moved from place to place.

But the Holy Places in which Jesus ministers is **the true tabernacle** of which the other was but a shadow. It is the heavenly tabernacle which the Lord, not man, **pitched.** This renders a verb meaning to fasten as with pegs. The aorist tense means that it was done once and never to be removed.

2. The Old Covenant (8:3–5)

While the word *covenant* is not used, these verses describe the tabernacle ministry under the old covenant which flows into the ministry of Jesus under the new. The thought is the superiority of the latter over the former.

For every high priest is ordained to offer gifts and sacrifices; wherefore it is of necessity that this man have somewhat also to offer (v.3).

Each high priest, Aaron and his successors, was appointed **to offer** (present infinitive) or bear forward gifts and sacrifices. The present tense shows the constant repetition of their work. It had to be done year after year.

This man should read "this one" with reference to Jesus. It means "this high priest" in contrast to those under the old covenant. Jesus as High Priest must also have something that he might offer. **To offer** here renders an aorist form. It speaks of *one* sacrifice on Jesus' part as over against the *many* sacrifices on the part of the other high priests.

For if he were on earth, he should not be a priest, seeing that there are priests that offer gifts according to the law (v.4).

Were Jesus on the earth, as opposed to the heavenly tabernacle, he would not even be a priest. He was not out of the tribe of Levi. Levitical priests were "the ones keeping on offering according to the law." Note the present participle expressing again the idea of continual offerings. There was no need for another priest under the old covenant. Even though its sacrifices did not effect a right relationship between God and man, still they were constantly being brought before God.

Who serve unto the example and shadow of heavenly things, as Moses was admonished of God when he was about to make the tabernacle: for, See, saith he, that thou make all things according to the pattern shewed to thee in the mount (v.5).

The priests under the old covenant served as a "copy" and **shadow** of the heavenly ministry of Jesus. Moffatt calls it "a shadowy outline." In this regard the author cited God's warning to Moses that he should make the tabernacle exactly like the "pattern" or type *(tupon)* shown to him while on Mount Sinai (cf. Ex. 25:40). Since the earthly tabernacle was to be a type of the heavenly one it was necessary that it be made with exactness. The author saw this exactness as also related to the priestly service since it was also a type of that which Jesus would perform in the true tabernacle.

3. The Better Covenant (8:6–7)

Thus the author passed from the *type* to the *true*. It served as a transition from the old to the new covenant.

But now hath he obtained a more excellent ministry, by how much also he is the mediator of a better covenant, which was established upon better promises (v.6).

Now brings the thought from the past to the present. Jesus has attained to **a more excellent ministry** than that of the high priest under the old covenant. This excellency extends to all that Jesus did/does.

Mediator (*mesitēs,* cf. 1 Tim. 2:5) means a middle man or arbitrator. When two parties had a difference a mediator was appointed to arbitrate their difference. He must perfectly represent both parties and do what was necessary to bring them to agreement.

As the God-Man, Jesus filled this role between God and man. He perfectly represented both, and in his atoning work provided the means necessary for reconciliation. Thus it is in Jesus' nature as both God and Man that they meet in reconciliation. This was done through the **better covenant** of grace rather than one of law.

It was a better covenant based upon **better promises,** which suggests its relation to God's covenant with Abraham (Gen. 12:1–3) rather than with the Mosaic covenant (Ex. 19:5–6). The former was unconditional (grace); the latter was conditional (law; cf. "if" and "then" in Ex. 19:5–6).

For if that first covenant had been faultless, then should no place have been sought for the second (v.7).

The old covenant with its if was a faulty one; the fault being Israel's weakness. Furthermore, its sacrificial system involved animals, not Jesus. And it was of law rather than of grace. All these things made it ineffective in carrying out God's redemptive purpose. So of necessity there had to be a new covenant which could fulfil God's will.

In the light of the purpose of the author in this epistle, it is well to note the idea of Jesus' work in reconciliation. Paul said that God having finished his reconciling work in Christ, "hath given to us the ministry of reconciliation . . . now we are ambassadors for [*huper,* on behalf of] Christ, as though God did beseech you by [*dia,* through] us: we pray you in Christ's stead [*huper Christou,* on behalf of, instead of Christ as his substitute or representative], be ye reconciled to God" (2 Cor. 5:18,20).

This is the equivalent of filling one's place in God's world-mission. The implication is that as Jesus has a more excellent ministry under a better covenant with better promises, to a corresponding degree is the responsibility of the Hebrew Christians over that of their Israelite forebears.

The good news of God in Christ would surpass the appeal of Mosaic law and ritual, and those who trusted the eternal High Priest would be obligated to share the gospel with all men.

4. The New Covenant (8:8–12)

After an introductory phrase the author, in verses 8–12, quoted Jeremiah 31:31–34. Jeremiah wrote these words against the background of God's impending judgment upon Judah for her rebellion against her covenant with Jehovah. Like Israel in the wilderness, that people would lose its opportunity. But God pointed to a time when a new covenant would be made with his people. The new covenant will be consummated in Jesus Christ.

For finding fault with them, he saith, Behold the days come, saith the Lord, when I will make a new covenant with the house of Israel and with the house of Judah (v.8).

At the outset it should be noted that God found fault not with the old covenant but with "them" or Israel. When they failed to keep the covenant of law, God made one of grace.

Will make renders *sunteleō*. It is an intensive form of *teleō*. It means fully to accomplish something. It has in it the thought of finality. God would make this new one and no other. It is his final overture to lost men. Since Israel had failed to keep the covenant of law he would make one of grace. What would men do with it?

Perhaps it will be helpful to examine more in detail *sunteleō*. *Teleō* is akin to *teleioō*. The latter verb speaks of the process of bringing something to its intended goal. In Hebrews 2:10 and 5:9 it is used of Jesus being made "perfect" or brought to his goal as Redeemer. But in 7:19 it is used of the law being unable to bring men into a right relation with God, which within itself made a new covenant necessary.

Teleō speaks of the final act in accomplishing that which is involved in *teleioō*. For instance, in John 19:28 both verbs are used. "After this, Jesus knowing that all things were now accomplished [*tetelestai*, perfect form of *teleō*], that the scripture might be fulfilled [*teleioō*], saith, I thirst." Jesus was ready to die. That would be the final act in bringing his atoning work to its intended end *(teleō)*. One thing yet remained to be fulfilled in the prophecies about his death. Psalm 22:15 spoke of the thirst of the suffering Christ. So not simply as a rote recitation but in agony, he said, "I thirst."

Actually this was to procure liquid that in full voice he might give the shout of victory—"It is finished" (John 19:30). This renders *tetelestai*, perfect form of *teleō*. That which had been in process of fulfilment or being brought to its desired end *(teleioō)*, the final act had been performed to complete it *(teleō)*.

The verb *teleo* does not appear in Hebrews, but *sunteleō* is its intensive form. So since the law could not complete the process necessary to bring men to God (7:19, *teleioō*). God gave a new covenant which could (8:8, *sunteleō*). Of course this verb relates to the actual giving of the new covenant. So his act in doing so was his final act in providing for man's redemption.

Note that this new covenant will be made with the **house of Israel** and the **house of Judah.** This suggests the divided kingdom following Solomon's reign.

Both houses had rebelled against the old covenant. So here the author spoke of both houses as comprising the new or true Israel, the Christian people (cf. 1 Peter 2:9–10). The Hebrew Christians were a part of this true Israel, as, indeed, are all who receive Christ. Even under the old covenant there had been a faithful remnant which comprised the true Israel. Paul discusses this matter in Romans 9–11. It is this true Israel that God would use in his world-mission (cf. Caleb and Joshua, Isaiah and Jeremiah, and all who are true to Jehovah).

Not according to the covenant that I made with their fathers in the day when I took them by the hand to lead them out of the land of Egypt; because they continued not in my covenant, and I regarded them not, saith the Lord" (v.9).

At this point it is well to look briefly at the covenant idea. It looms large in the life of all ancient peoples. The Hebrew word for covenant is *berîth* (Greek, *diathēkē*) which comes from a verb akin to the Assyrian word *barû,* to bind. So a covenant was binding. However, the Hebrew word carries the root idea "to cut." It expressed the custom of cutting a covenant in stone. Some see also the practice of cutting the body to get blood with which to seal the agreement between the two parties. A covenant was a legal agreement (cf. Heb. 9:16 f.) which, when sealed, was binding on the parties to it. It could not be broken without penalty.

Covenants between equals were equally binding upon both parties. But when made between a superior and an inferior party, the former made conditions which must be kept by the latter before the superior party was bound by his part of the agreement. Obviously a covenant between God and man fell into this class. However, the superior one might also make a covenant which contained no conditions. Such would be the covenants which he made with Adam (Gen. 3:15), Noah (Gen. 9:8 ff.), and Abraham (Gen. 12:1–3; cf. 26:2 ff.; 28:13 ff.).

However, the covenant made with Israel through Moses was a conditional covenant. It was this covenant which the author of Hebrews had in mind in 8:9.

When Moses was in the midst of his contest with Pharaoh, God gave him instructions to pass on to Israel. "I am the Lord, and I will bring you out from under the burdens of the Egyptians, and I will rid you out of their bondage, and *I will redeem you* . . . and I will take you to me for a people, and I will be to you a God . . . and I will bring you in unto the land, concerning the which I did swear to give it to Abraham, to Isaac, and to Jacob" (Ex. 6:7 f., author's italics).

Notice that this covenant was related to God carrying out the one made with Abraham. That covenant was one of grace with no conditions attached. It inaugurated historically God's redemptive mission. It was a covenant of grace, sealed not in animal's blood but in the blood of Christ (cf. Heb. 9:15 ff.). In Israel's case God kept that covenant in redeeming Israel out of Egyptian bondage.

Three months later at Mount Sinai God proposed to enter into a covenant with Israel as a nation. It is important in understanding Hebrews to remember that this was a covenant with a *redeemed people.* So in the author's mind the problem of the covenant had nothing to do with Israel's redemption or that of his readers. It related to what a redeemed people should do in sharing God's redemptive purpose.

The covenant at Mount Sinai was a conditional covenant of service. God began by reminding Israel that they were a redeemed people, redeemed out of the bondage of Egypt (Ex. 19:3–4). In the mind of the author of Hebrews this redemption corresponded to his readers' redemption from sin. In both cases these redemptions were mighty works of God through the faith of the recipients. They were redeemed not "out of" themselves or good works but "out of God"—"unto good works" (cf. Eph. 2:8–10).

"Now therefore [because they were a redeemed people], *if* ye will obey my voice indeed, and keep my covenant, *then* ye shall be a peculiar treasure unto me above all people: for all the earth is mine: and ye shall be unto me a kingdom of priests, and an holy nation" (Ex. 19:5–6, author's italics).

As a peculiar treasure God would use them as no other people. They would be a priest-nation, holy or set apart to God's service, but note the "if" and "then." God had redeemed them, and would give them a land from which to carry out the covenant. But if they were to be a priest-nation they must keep the "if." Only "then" was God obligated to retain them as his peculiar treasure as a dedicated priest-nation. And Israel accepted the terms of the covenant (Ex. 5:8).

The author of Hebrews said that this covenant was faulty (8:7). And the Old Testament echoes this tragic truth. To begin with Israel rebelled at Kadesh-barnea. When Joshua took another generation into Canaan they failed to rid the land of the Canaanites. Thus, rather than to *evangelize* the Canaanites, she became paganized by them; the book of Judges tells the bitter story. Israel sinned, God punished, Israel repented, God delivered. It was the same old story. Rather than to be a priest-nation Israel shamed God by turning to paganism.

What was the basic reason for Israel's failure as a priest-nation? She forgot her spiritual mission in pursuit of worldly goals. In 1 Samuel 8 her leaders requested a king in place of the theocratic rule of Jehovah. To Samuel the leaders said, **Make us a king to judge us like all the nations** (v.5). Like all the nations instead of being a *peculiar treasure, a priest-nation, a dedicated nation.* They wanted a king that **we may be like all the nations; and that our king may judge us, and go out before us, and** *fight our battles* (vv. 19 f.; author's italics).

Two things are clear. They wanted to imitate their pagan neighbors instead of being a people of God. They measured greatness by pagan standards, not by God's standards (cf. Matt. 20:25–28). And they thought in terms of military conquests rather than a spiritual crusade. God said that they had not rejected Samuel; they had rejected him. Here was the rebellion of Kadesh-barnea all over again.

It is a tragic thing when God's people become so involved in seeking earthly fame, glory, power, and wealth that they neglect the very reason for their being. Who can estimate the souls lost from God because of this attitude through the centuries—even today!

Down the years as Israel and Judah pursued their worldly goals, God continually sent prophets to call them back from pagan ways to their covenant relation. But to no avail. It was when Judah faced the Babylonian captivity that God through Jeremiah announced his new covenant.

This covenant was to be realized in Jesus Christ. As the old covenant had been sealed in animal's blood (Ex. 24:8), so the new was sealed in Jesus' blood (Heb. 9:15 ff.). Thus as a redeemed people the Hebrew Christians stood in a new covenant relation with God.

For this is the covenant that I will make with the house of Israel after those days, saith the Lord; I will put my laws into their mind, and write them in their hearts: and I will be to them a God, and they shall be to me a people (v.10).

Note here that it is **the house of Israel,** a united people under God's rule, the ideal which God had chosen in Egypt. Rather than law written on tablets of stone, they will be written "in their mind . . . in their hearts." Aristotle used "mind" in the sense of all the intellect or understanding. In this sense here a moral understanding. Westcott calls the heart the seat of man's personal life. *Heart* may also be seen as the seat of the will. So *mind* and *heart* include all of man's inner nature.

"I will be to them a God, and they shall be to me a people" reflects Exodus 6:7. What God intended before Israel's redemption out of Egypt will be realized through Christ under the new covenant. Israel had failed to be a "peculiar treasure" unto God. So he will provide it in the true Israel. God may change his people but never his purpose. If one people will not fulfil his world-mission he will provide another.

And they shall not teach every man his neighbour, and every man his brother, saying, Know the Lord: for all shall know me, from the least to the greatest (v.11).

This does not mean that there will be no need for evangelism under the new covenant. The point is the condition of close relationship between the Lord and those in the new covenant.

Under this new covenant there will be no need for a priest to teach the details of the law. Dods notes that under the law only the highly trained scribe could understand "the minutiae of the law with which religion was identified. The elaborate ritual made it impossible for the private individual to know whether a ram or a pigeon was the appropriate sacrifice for his sin, or whether his sin was mortal or venial. A priest had to be consulted. Under the new covenant intermediates were to be abolished." [2]

Here then is *the priesthood of believers.* And with the privileges of such there were/are responsibilities of sharing the gospel with a lost world.

Note the word **know** in verse 11. The former renders *ginōskō,* to know by experience or to recognize. It is an aorist tense, suggesting the idea of bringing someone for the first time to know the Lord. Those who have through faith in Christ come under the new covenant will not need this. For "they shall know me." Here "know" renders the perfect tense of *oida,* to know with perception or with a soul-knowledge. Those in Christ will *fully know* the Lord.

Not teach has the strong double negative *ou mē*. It expresses strongly the fact that all under the new covenant will have a full-knowledge of God. The reason is that God will in Christ be merciful to their unrighteousness, **and their sins . . . . will I remember no more. And their iniquities** is not in the best texts. **No more** is another strong double negative *ou mē*. Under this covenant of grace God not only forgives sin but most surely does not call to mind that which he has forgiven. This is because of Jesus' once-for-all sacrifice which makes others unnecessary.

Well and good! The readers of this epistle had this assurance. But if they were to fulfil the obligation of this covenant, they must share it with a lost world. This covenant has better promises. And as Abraham's seed are blessed they are to be a blessing.

It is vitally necessary to keep the covenant idea in a proper focus. Abraham's covenant was unconditional, by grace, and, it pointed to Christ (cf. Gal. 3:14,16). It was one of redemption and which promised a land whence his spiritual seed could be a blessing to all the earth. This is seen by the author of Hebrews typically in Israel's redemption from Egypt and being deposited in the Promised Land whence she was to carry out the covenant as a priest-nation as evidenced by the Mosaic covenant. It was thus that she was to be a blessing. Actually the Abrahamic covenant was fulfilled in Christ, and involved the Hebrew Christians as a redeemed and sanctified people, dedicated as God's priest-nation under the new covenant.

To understand the author's point one must see it in the light of Jesus' words in Matthew 21:33–43. The parable of the wicked husbandmen depicts Israel's repeated rebellion against God's redemptive mission. It was climaxed in her rejection and crucifixion of God's Son, Abraham's true Seed. On this basis Jesus said, "The kingdom of God shall be taken from you, and given to a nation bringing forth the fruits thereof" (Matt. 21:43). The chief priests and Pharisees, representatives of this rebellious nation, perceived that he spoke of them (v.45).

First Peter 2:4–10 completes the picture. Compare the wording of this passage with Exodus 19:5–6 and Matthew 21:43–44. It is clear that the apostle had these in mind. He was saying that his readers, Christians, stood in the same relation to God as had Israel under the old covenant. They are "a chosen generation, a peculiar people: *that ye should shew forth the praises of him who hath called you out of darkness into his marvellous light*" (1 Peter 2:9, author's italics). In time past they were not a people, "but are now the people of God" (v.10).

No longer does God's redemptive mission run through a constituted nation such as ancient Israel. It now runs through a people who were not a constituted nation. They have been redeemed "out of every kindred, and tongue, and people, and nation" (Rev. 5:9) to become the people of God.

This fits in with the author's various warnings that the Hebrew Christians should not, through rebellion against God's world-mission, let happen to them what happened to national Israel. And the same warning extends to every

Christian. Not a loss of redemption provided through the unconditional Abrahamic covenant of grace, but a loss of opportunity involved in the conditional Mosaic covenant of service.

5. The Transition from the Old to the New Covenant (8:13)

In that he saith, A new covenant, he hath made the first old. Now that which decayeth and waxeth old is ready to vanish away.

The coming in of a new, fresh covenant through Jesus made the former one old. **Hath made old** renders the perfect form of a verb meaning to treat as old and out of date. This is completely true of the Mosaic covenant. **Decayeth and waxeth old** emphasizes the contrast with the new, fresh covenant.

The old is **ready to vanish away.** Actually it is "nigh to disappearing." The old covenant with its ineffective rituals and sacrifices was almost gone. Actually it was fulfilled in Christ. But since the author did not say, "Has vanished away," he was not thinking of that.

This statement probably refers to the destruction of Jerusalem and the temple in A.D. 70. Apparently it had not happened. Or else again the author would have said, "Has vanished away." Such would have been a strong point in his argument. But he said that it was about to vanish. So evidently he was writing before A.D. 70, but not long before. It appears that he was aware of the desperate situation in Jerusalem. It was only a matter of time until the city would fall. Due to the long siege of the city and the ferocity of the struggle he could well foresee the bloody carnage described by Josephus when Jerusalem finally fell. Save for Herod's palace the city, its walls, and temple were leveled with the ground. Archaelogists are now probing into the ashes and rubble of that destroyed city. Herod's palace served as quarters for troops left to guard the site to see that the city was not rebuilt.

But the author was not writing history in advance. His concern was the system of rituals and ceremonies under the old covenant. He saw this system about to disappear in fact as it already had in meaning.

History records that with the fall of Jerusalem and the temple, center of Judaism's power, Christianity was loosed from any bonds with Judaism. Up to that time it had been regarded by the world as just another branch of Judaism. But then it was loosed upon the world in a new dimension. Its message was regarded even by the Romans as a new message of a new movement. It was probably to this that Jesus referred when he spoke of "the kingdom of God come with power" (Mark 9:1).

If these things be regarded as true then this constitutes another reminder to the Hebrew Christians of the opportunity and responsibility which challenged them to faithfulness in God's world-mission of redemption. It abides as a challenge to God's people in every age.

As these Hebrew Christians contemplated the approaching holocaust in Palestine their hearts must have been deeply stirred, even as Christians today view the world scene. But in each case the time was/is not one of fear or of turning aside from their world-mission. The very trying times call them to renewed vigor on the Lord's behalf.

Someone said that when the world is at its worst, Christian people must be at their best.

Notes

1. *The Expositor's Greek Testament,* "Hebrews," Eerdmans, Grand Rapids, 1951, p. 320; cf. Robertson, *op. cit.,* p. 388.
2. *Op. cit.,* p. 325.

IX. The Mediator of the New Covenant

In 8:6 the author referred to Jesus as "the mediator of a better covenant." Chapter 9 develops this idea as the author compared the sacrificial ministry of the old covenant with the new.

1. The Imperfect Mediation (9:1-10)

Then verily the first covenant had also ordinances of divine service, and a worldly sanctuary. For there was a tabernacle made; the first, wherein was the candlestick, and the table, and the shewbread; which is called the sanctuary (vv. 1-2).

Under the old covenant, worship centered in the tabernacle, an ornate tent oblong in shape. It had been made by Moses and his helpers out of materials supplied by the people (Ex. 25:1 ff.). It was symbolic of Jehovah's presence with his people (v.8). The author of Hebrews called it **a worldly sanctuary** or one related to this world (v.1). This was in contrast to the heavenly sanctuary in which Jesus ministers as High Priest (cf. 8:5 f.).

In the sanctuary itself were the Holy Place and the Holy of Holies (vv. 2-3). In the Holy Place were certain objects which symbolized certain relations which God had with his people. **The candlestick** or lampstand made of pure gold was for the practical purpose of giving light inside the windowless tent. But it also symbolized that God was Israel's light, a light which she was to share with the world.

There was also the table of shewbread. The table was made of acacia wood overlaid with gold. On it was the shewbread; twelve cakes, one for each tribe. This bread was renewed by the priests weekly. It reminded Israel that God was her life, a life that also she was to share with other nations.

The author did not mention the altar of incense which stood before the inner veil separating the Holy Place from the Holy of Holies. Continuously burning incense was a symbol of the prayers which went up to God.

The choice of the candlestick and the shewbread suggests that the author was primarily concerned to point out those things which symbolized Israel's light and life, both of which she was to share with pagan people. This was related to her world-mission.

And after the second veil, the tabernacle which is called the Holiest of all (v.3).

The first veil led into the Holy Place. The second veil led from there into the "Holiest of all," literally, "the Holy of Holies." It was in the Holy of Holies that God was said to dwell in mercy with his people. This second veil suggests the inapproachable nature of God.

Which had a golden censer, and the ark of the covenant overlaid round about with gold, wherein was the golden pot that had manna, and Aaron's rod that budded, and the tables of the covenant; and over it the cherubims of glory shadowing the mercy-seat; of which we cannot now speak particularly (vv. 4–5).

Within the veil in the Holy of Holies also there were certain items. The author placed the **golden censer** in the Holy of Holies. This has been a problem to interpreters. Even though Exodus 30: 6–7 is indefinite as to its exact location, the evidence seems to be that it was outside the inner veil. For Aaron was to burn incense on it daily. He entered into the Holy of Holies only on the Day of Atonement (9:7). Robertson notes the dual use of the word rendered **golden censer.** In the Septuagint it is translated *censer* (2 Chron. 26:19). However, Philo and Josephus used it for the altar of incense. Some see the evidence to favor the meaning "altar of incense." However, others see it as the censer which Aaron took with him annually when he entered the Holy of Holies (cf. Lev. 16:12 f.). Apparently this thought was uppermost in the author's mind.

The "ark of the covenant" was a small container overlaid within and without with pure gold. In the ark were three objects. There was the golden pot of manna (cf. Ex. 16) which reminded Israel of God's sustenance during her wilderness sojourn. There was also "Aaron's rod that budded" (Num. 17:10). It suggested his divine appointment as Israel's high priest whose ministry preserved them and made them acceptable to God for his service. The third object was the two tables of stone, **tables of the covenant,** on which were written the Ten Commandments (cf. Ex. 24:12; 25:16). These tablets were constant reminders of Israel's covenant of service with Jehovah (cf. Ex. 19:5–9; 24:1–8).

Over this ark was laid the mercy seat, a slab of pure gold, which was to be the meeting place between God and Moses (cf. Ex. 25:17,22). Overshadowing the mercy seat were "the cherubims of glory" (cf. Ex. 18 ff.). This suggested God's presence in mercy.

Of which we cannot now speak particularly. The author did not propose to go into further details as to these objects. He described them generally simply to set the stage for his contrast between the ministry of Aaron and Jesus respectively. And to that purpose he moved immediately.

Now when these things were thus ordained, the priests went always into the first tabernacle, accomplishing the service of God (v.6).

After the tabernacle had been built and furnished, the Levitical priests ministered daily in the Holy Place. Daily offerings were made as individuals brought their sacrifices for their sins or various other gift offerings. Also on set occasions throughout the year they rendered other priestly services (cf. Num. 28-29): the daily burnt offering (28:3); offerings on the sabbath (28:9), the new year (28:11), the Passover (28:16), the day of the first fruits (28:26), the feast of trumpets

(29:1), and at other occasions.

The purpose of the author was to point out the succession of sacrifices by a constantly changing priesthood—generation after generation. The word **always** renders *dia pantos. Pantos* without the definite article means all things in their several parts. So it was *through (dia)* an endless ritual in its several parts that the priests ministered. Also in the author's mind was the ineffectiveness of these sacrifices to make the people permanently pure for God's service.

But into the second went the high priest alone once each year, not without blood, which he offered for himself, and for the errors of the people (v.7).

This refers to the service of the high priest on the annual Day of Atonement. It was an atonement made annually "throughout your generations" (cf. Ex. 30:10). It also had to be repeated year after year. Leviticus 16 describes in detail how this was to be done.

On this day, after washing himself, the high priest put on linen garments called "holy garments" (v.4). Then he selected a bullock and two goats for a sin offering, and one ram for a burnt offering. One goat was to be sacrificed and the other was to be a "scapegoat." The one was sacrificial, as a sin offering; the other was presented alive before the Lord.

First, Aaron sacrificed the bullock as a sin offering for himself and his house. Then taking the bullock's blood and a censer he entered the Holy of Holies. The cloud of incense covered the mercy seat that Aaron might not die. He could enter God's presence only by blood and in prayer. Then he sprinkled the mercy seat with the bullock's blood and seven times before the mercy seat. This was for his own sins.

After this he went out into the Holy Place and sacrificed the goat as a sin offering for the people. Reentering the Holy of Holies with its blood, he sprinkled it on and before the mercy seat as he had done with the blood of the bullock.

Then Aaron took the blood of both the bullock and goat out into the Holy Place and sprinkled both upon the horns of the altar. This was done as an atonement for the Holy Place itself. Thus he hallowed it from the uncleanness of the children of Israel (v.19).

Having done this, he took the scapegoat and symbolically placed on it the sins of the people. The goat was then led into the wilderness bearing away the sins of the people. The one leading the goat away was required to wash his clothes and body before reentering the camp.

Aaron went into the tabernacle of the congregation, took off his linen garments, and left them there. In the Holy Place he washed his body, put on his clothes, and made a burnt offering for the people. Thus he made atonement for both himself and the people. The fatty portions of the sin offering were burned on the altar.

The remainder of the bullock and goat for the sin offering was carried outside the camp and burned (cf. Heb. 13:11). The man doing this also washed his clothes and body before reentering the camp.

God commanded that this Day of Atonement should be observed by Aaron and his successors year after year (cf. Lev. 16:29–34). As one can see, this was all highly symbolic. At the end of the entire ceremony the high priest coming again among the people was evidence that atonement for sin had been made for another year. And they went abroad sharing the good news.

Now the author set forth the lesson gained from the reference to the high priest's ministry on the Day of Atonement.

The Holy Ghost [Spirit] this signifying [making plain, cf. 12:27], **that the way into the holiest of all was not yet made manifest, while as the first tabernacle was yet standing** (v.8).

Because the high priest could not enter the Holy of Holies without animal's blood, it was evident that the way into the presence of God was not yet made perfectly plain **(made manifest)**. This was true so long as the first tabernacle, symbolic of the old covenant, still had a place in God's dealings with men. The people could not even enter the Holy Place. The priests could not go beyond that place. Only the high priest could enter the Holy of Holies (symbolic of God's presence, cf. vv. 12,25), and that annually and only with the blood of animal sacrifice and in prayer.

Which was a figure for the time then present, in which were offered both gifts and sacrifices, that could not make him that did the service perfect, as pertaining to the conscience; which stood only in meats and drinks, and divers washings, and carnal ordinances, imposed on them until the time of reformation (vv. 9–10).

Which or "which very thing" refers to the tabernacle and its services. They are but **a figure.** The Greek word is *parabolē*, parable. It means a casting alongside. Someone defined a parable as an earthly story with a heavenly meaning. And as a handle by which to pick up and carry home spiritual truth. It cast earthly things alongside spiritual truth to enable one to understand the latter. In a sense the reference here corresponds to "example" *(tupon)* in 8:5.

This *parable* could not make perfect or complete the conscience of the one rendering the service, either the high priest or the people on whose behalf he functioned before the altar. **Gifts** along with **sacrifices** could extend this to include the day-by-day ministry of the priests. Such things affected only the outward relation of the people to being a part of the commonwealth of Israel. They effected no inner change.

The reason being that they centered only in dietary laws **(meats and drinks,** clean and unclean), ceremonial ablutions **(divers washings,** note washings by the high priest and others), and ordinances related to the flesh. In these words the author expanded the thought beyond the Day of Atonement to include the entire legal system under the old covenant.

So by their very nature these things involved in the *parable* pointed to a time of fulfilment in the *true.* The type and shadow (cf. 8:5) must give way to the reality.

This the author called **the time of reformation. Time** *(kairon)* means the opportune time, a time of God's own choosing. **Reformation** renders a word which means to set right or straight. It is *diorthōsis* from *diorthoō* whence comes the English word *orthopedics.* Hippocrates used this verb for making straight misshapen limbs. So "the time of the reformation" is a time when God made straight his redemptive revelation in Christ.

This speaks of the inadequacy of the old system. It was an ineffective mediator between God and men. But it was a *parable* pointing to the true spiritual meaning of the sacrifice made by Christ. It was to this fulfilment that the author now turned.

2. The Perfect Mediator (9:11-15)

All that was typified in the old covenant system of sacrifice was fulfilled in Christ. This the author showed as he referred to both the tabernacle and the sacrifice.

But Christ being come an high priest of good things to come, by a greater and more perfect tabernacle, not made with hands, that is to say, not of this building (v.11).

But introduces the contrast between the old and the new. In the Greek text **Christ** is the first word in the sentence, so emphatic. Christ's coming made the difference. **Being come** renders an aorist participle which reads better as "having." It refers to the historical fact of his incarnation, which, of course, includes all of his redeeming work in history. He was eternally High Priest. So he was manifested as such in the arena of history. He stands at the heart of history both time wise and redemption wise. Only in the light of redemptive history can one understand history as such (cf. Rev. 5:9-13).

Of good things to come poses a problem. Does it mean good things *about* to come *(mellontōn,* as read in two strong manuscripts, Aleph and A)? Or does it mean good things already realized in the event of his coming *(genomenōn,* as found in other strong texts, B and D)? Westcott favors the latter; Moffatt follows the former. Robertson agrees with Moffatt, but points out that both meanings are true. The **good things** had already been provided by God and only awaited the fulfilment of divine conditions wherein they could be experienced. And they also point to the full experience of them in the blessed hope of the Lord's return (cf. 9:28). Grant follows *mellontōn* in the text, but footnotes the other reading. Dods does likewise. However, he notes that "more probably the writer has in view the slender benefits obtained by the Levitical High Priest, and contrasts them with the illimitable good mediated through Christ." [1]

Thomas is helpful at this point.

This implies, not that Christ has become a High Priest of "the good things that are certain to come," but of "the good things which have already come." It is difficult to say which is the correct view, especially since from different standpoints both are true. In support of the contention that Christ is the priest of things yet to come in the future, it is rightly argued that the Epistle is always pointing forward. On the other hand, Nairne and others maintain that the change from "things already come" to "things certain to come" is too obvious to be true, and that the whole idea requires the thought of the good things as already provided in Christ. . . . But in any case the "good things" referred to have already been realized, at least in part, by means of the Incarnation and Priesthood of Christ.[2]

This writer agrees as to the difficulty of choosing between the two ideas. For certainly both are possible. Actually in the broadest sense "the good things" were provided in eternity, wrought out in history, and point to a full realization beyond this age. But was the author pointing to the future primarily? In the sense of a full salvation—regeneration, sanctification, glorification—the future is always in the picture.

However, the author's primary purpose at a given point will be seen in the light of one's overall view of Hebrews. This writer sees that purpose primarily related to the *present*. Because of what God in Christ has done for the readers, and with a view to final glorification, what should they do in their present state of regeneration and sanctification? The call is to present faithfulness in God's world-mission. So in this sense the primary probability is that the author referred to the good things already realized. The eternal purpose to provide redemption became a historical reality in the redemptive work of Christ, at the point of the writing of this epistle that had already come. It was a reality which but waited for its propagation to fulfil God's redemptive purpose.

Christ had provided this redemption by his ministry in the heavenly tabernacle, which involved a better sacrifice—that of himself.

Neither by the blood of goats and calves, but by his own blood he entered once into the holy place, having obtained eternal redemption for us (v.12).

Christ's sacrifice was better by the same degree as his own blood is over that of animals. Aaron offered animal sacrifice. Christ is both High Priest and Sacrifice. Whereas Aaron bore animal blood into the earthly Holy of Holies annually, Christ bore his own blood into the heavenly Holy of Holies **once** *(ephapax)* or "once for all." There is no need for other atoning work. In the Greek text **the holy place** renders *ta hagia,* plural, the holy places. Aaron made the sacrifice in the Holy Place and from there bore it into the Holy of Holies. So Christ was sacrificed on earth and bore his blood from there into the heavenly Holy of Holies.

It was to the end that he might provide "of the ages redemption." **For us** is not in the original text. He provided redemption. What man does with it is up to him. It was not a *year-by-year* redemption but eternal redemption, and so needing no repeating.

Redemption was the price paid to free a captive or slave. But, of course, one should not see in this that God paid a ransom to Satan, else Satan would be more powerful than God. The redemption wrought in Christ was paid to God himself in that by it he provided the condition under which he could pardon sin. He became both "just, and the justifier of him which believeth in Jesus" (Rom. 3:26). In his sinless life Jesus proved God "just" in his demand for righteousness in man. Then in Jesus' death God became the "justifier" of all who through faith receive this righteousness through Christ.

One may ask why Christ's blood could do what animal blood could not do?

Man is a person. Animals are dumb brutes. They were unwilling sacrifices with no understanding of what was involved in their death. But Jesus, a person, willingly gave himself in full awareness of what his death meant for lost men. So through faith in him there is an interplay of persons which is necessary for man's salvation.

Why did God wait so long to provide this redemption in Christ? He knew that the blood of animals could not bring man into a right relation with him. But man did not know it. It was only after he realized the inefficacy of repeated animal sacrifices that he was conditioned to trust in the blood of Christ.

For if the blood of bulls and of goats, and the ashes of an heifer sprinkling the unclean, sanctifieth to the purifying of the flesh: how much more shall the blood of Christ, who through the eternal Spirit offered himself without spot to God, purge your conscience from dead works to serve the living God? (vv. 13–14).

Here the author argued from the lesser to the greater. It should be remembered that the old covenant rituals were designed to *purify* God's people that they might be fit instruments for his service. This involved both the sacrifice on the annual Day of Atonement and also the intermediate cleansings necessary to keep one a fit vessel of service.

These verses involve both. The Day of Atonement is seen in **the blood of bulls and of goats.** But what about the **ashes of an heifer?** This refers to Numbers 19. If an Israelite touched a dead body he was unclean for seven days (v.11; cf. also vv. 14–18). Such was cut off from the congregation of Israel, the covenant people, if he remained unclean beyond seven days. Thus he was unfit to serve God as a part of the covenant people. To provide cleansing in such cases a red heifer, without blemish and having never worn a yoke, was slain. Its blood was sprinkled before the tabernacle seven times. Then the heifer's body was burned. The ashes were kept and as needed were mixed with water. The defiled person to be purified must sprinkle himself with this water on the third day. Then on the seventh day he was clean or sanctified. He was fit both to commune with and serve God. If he did not sprinkle himself, he was not clean on the seventh day. This was used by the author to show the necessity of occasional cleansing other than on the Day of Atonement. And this to the end that he might be a part of the priest-nation and its divine mission.

Contrariwise, the atonement wrought by Christ cleansed one once for all. There was no need for other cleansings. The moment one believes in him he is both regenerated and sanctified. He is kept so by the "eternal redemption" provided by Christ. Like the unblemished heifer, Christ, through the Holy Spirit, presented himself without spot before God as the once-for-all Sacrifice. Thus he makes clean the **conscience,** the sum-total of the inner man, **from dead works to serve the living God.**

How may one understand **dead works?** Obviously the contrast is between *dead bodies* and *dead works.* Dods suggests a pause before **works,** "from dead—not bodies—but works." As the sprinkling of the ashes of the heifer cleansed from association with dead bodies and things connected with them, so Christ cleanses permanently from dead works.

Paul speaks of "wicked works" (Col. 1:21). This means those deeds which are essentially wrong. But **dead works** suggests *good works* which have no spiritual vitality or purpose. Many things which are good within themselves have no relation to God's redemptive purpose and mission. To give all of one's time and energy to these to the neglect of one's place in God's spiritual ministry is to be defiled by dead works. This cuts the Christian off from his responsibility in God's missionary purpose for his people.

Now the author said that Christ's atonement cleanses the Christian from such. Though such may at times act *unsaintly* he is still a *saint.* He is a *holy one,* set apart, dedicated, sanctified for God's service.

This focuses attention on **to serve the living god.** Literally, "unto [*eis*] the to serve a living God." *Eis* here expresses purpose or goal. The purpose of one's redemption is that he should serve a living God, not be absorbed in dead works or works unrelated to the purposes of this living God. Paul expressed it in Ephesians 2:10: "Created in Christ Jesus unto [*epi*] good works, which God hath before ordained that we should walk in them." Good works here do not mean good-for-nothing works. They are *good* because they fit into God's purpose. *Epi,* for, followed by the dative case of purpose expresses the purpose of this new creation in Christ.[3] However, for one to fulfil his place in this state of sanctification he must experience spiritual renewal as he confesses to Christ sins of disobedience (cf. 1 John 1:9).

Here then is another challenge and encouragement with respect to the readers' world-mission. They had no excuse for not fulfilling it.

And for this cause he is the mediator of the new testament, that by means of death, for the redemption of the transgressions that were under the first testament, that they which are called might receive the promise of eternal inheritance (v.15).

It is for this very cause that Christ is the **mediator** (cf. 8:6) of the new covenant. **Testament** renders *diathēkē* used for covenant. The translators probably used **testament** here in anticipation of verses 16–17. But here the author was still thinking of the contrast between the old and new covenants. **By means of death** reads, "by means of a death having taken place." This, of course, refers to the death of Christ.

And what was the cause? That in his death Christ might make effective the sacrifices under the old covenant. The value in the sacrifices under the old covenant found their fulfilment in the death of Christ. So this means that those who were saved under the old covenant were saved through faith looking forward to the cross, as those since that event do so by looking back in faith to it. This does not mean that all Israelites under the old covenant were saved. It was they who in faith regarded the sacrifices as pointing to a greater work of God. They saw not merely the death of animals, but that somehow in God's own way death of the substitute sufficed for them.

God has but one plan of salvation for both Jew and Gentile. Peter stated it in Acts 15:11. "But we believe that through the grace of our Lord Jesus Christ we [Jews] shall be saved, even as they [Gentiles]." Christ's atonement did not suffice for all Israelites even as it does not today for all Gentiles. The author of Hebrews said that God's redemptive purpose did not relate to a commonwealth but to individual persons.

They which are called must be read in the light of the universal invitation for men to receive Christ. It renders a perfect passive participle meaning a complete call. God offers his redemption to all men. Those who accept it are *the called.*

Some see this otherwise, as referring to certain individuals to the exception of others. Such a position magnifies God's sovereignty, but ignores man's free will. They are in seeming conflict. However, God's sovereignty means that he acts within himself with no needed authority or power outside himself. However, by his own self-limitation he does not act contrary to his own nature and purpose. God is love, an attribute which colors all other of his attributes. As saving love he wills to save all men, but also in keeping with his nature and purpose. In his atoning work through Christ he has provided grounds upon which he can forgive sin. But he can forgive only those who in faith receive his offer. Or else he would violate his nature as holiness, righteousness, and truth.

So "the called" suggests God's purpose in election (cf. Eph. 1:3–14). He has as sovereign God elected to save all who are *in Christ.* By the act of his free will man determines whether or not he is *in Christ.* God did not save Israel *en masse.* He saved those who in faith looked forward to the supreme Sacrifice. The very covenant with Israel shows that God would extend his grace to other than Israel.

Which suggests another facet to *election.* God elected a *plan* of salvation. He also elected a *people* to propagate that plan. The *people* under the new covenant are those who through faith in Christ have become a part of the true Israel (cf. 1 Pet. 2:4–10).

So the perfect Mediator has made it possible for God and man to meet in reconciliation. It should be noted that God needs no reconciliation to man, else there would be no redemptive purpose. The call is not "God be reconciled to man!" It is "Be ye reconciled to God" (2 Cor. 5:20). And God was in Christ making possible that reconciliation.

3. The New Testament and the Testator (9:16–17)

In verse 15 the author had spoken of **the promise of eternal inheritance.** And this suggested the figure of a **testament** or will. Therefore, beginning here and going through verse 22 the author drew his contrast of the two systems from that point of view.

For where a testament is, there must also of necessity be the death of the testator (v.16).

This is an obvious fact. The word rendered **testament** is the same one for *covenant (diathēkē).* Moulton and Milligan point out that in the papyri and inscriptions "the word means *testament, will,* with absolute unanimity." [4] The word *adiathetos* is used for *intestate.* The readers would be familiar with this legal usage as well as the biblical one.

The idea of inheritance with respect to the Christian experience is widely seen in the New Testament (cf. Rom. 8:17 f.). To carry out the legal sense Christ put all believers in his *will* for eternal life, a quality of life beginning now and continuing in eternity. Such a will can become effective only upon the death of the "testator," in this case, Christ.

For a testament is of force after men are dead: otherwise it is of no strength at all while the testator liveth (v.17).

Of force translates *bebaia,* meaning a guarantee (cf. 3:6,14). Actually, "For a will upon death is guaranteed." So long as the testator lives the will is inoperative. Even though a child is in his father's will for a legacy, he cannot claim it until his father dies. The father, while living, might change or cancel it; but once the father dies, the terms of the will are guaranteed. One should not press this point to saying that Christ might change or cancel his will. The author's primary thought is that Christ died in order to make his will effective, so that all who believe in him should not perish, but have everlasting life (cf. John 3:16 ff.).

This is not an isolated instance of a legal figure depicting the redemptive work of Christ. One may see such in Jesus' word on the cross, "It is finished" (John 19:30, *tetelestai*). In the life of that day *teleō* was used in a legal and commercial sense. One usage was that of paying taxes or rent for the privilege of living in a country or house. Another was in connection with a promissory note. Receipts were often introduced with the word *tetelestai,* the very word Jesus used on the cross. Applying these senses, when Jesus died he paid the price for believers to live in God's kindgom and/or house. He fully paid his promissory note to save all who receive him. Or in the same sense he signed a receipt for the payment on behalf of all believers of their debt of sin against God.[5]

It is clear, therefore, that in his death Jesus made provision for those who are heirs of God and joint-heirs with Christ. Here again is the idea of partnership expressed in 3:1 and 6:4.

4. The Old Testament and Its Testator (9:18-22)

By contrast the Old Testament or covenant also was sealed in blood, animals' blood (v.18). With what Moffatt calls "characteristic freedom" the author made reference to the sealing of the old covenant (vv. 19–21; cf. Ex. 24:3–8).

This is the blood of the testament which God hath enjoined unto you (v.20). The author parallels Jesus' words in Mark 14:24. So one may see a kinship in Jesus' mind with Exodus 24:8

And almost all things are by the law purged with blood; and without shedding of blood is no remission (v.22). **Almost** renders an old adverb *schedon* which may read, "I may almost say." Fire and water were used for purging (cf. Ex. 19:10; Lev. 15:5; Num. 16:46 f.; 31:23 f.). But these things did not weaken the author's statement. The Greek text reads "in the sphere of [*en*] blood" not **with blood.** It is placed in the emphatic position. According to the Mosaic law **all**

things (*panta*, including men as well as things) are made clean in the sphere of blood. And apart from the shedding or pouring out of blood there is no carrying away of sin.

A physician recently told the writer that medical science has discovered that blood is the most effective cleansing agent. However, the author's meaning goes even beyond physical to spiritual cleansing. Sophisticated men may object to a *bloody* religion. But God does not.

Even so, the blood of animals was only a shadow pointing to the blood of Christ, the "blood of the new testament, which is shed for many for the remission of sins" (Matt. 26:28). This shedding of Jesus' blood was necessary, or else God would not have willed it.

5. The Once-for-all Sacrifice (9:23–28)

Here again the author showed the relation between the old covenant sacrifices and the death of Christ. The former but pointed to the latter.

It was therefore necessary that the patterns [copies] of things in the heavens should be purified with these; but the heavenly things themselves with better sacrifices than these (v.23).

The tabernacle and its furnishings and ceremonies were but copies of the heavenly reality. They were purified with animal blood. But the heavenly with **better sacrifices,** that of Christ. The plural form was used for the general idea. But as a matter of fact all of the sacrifices in the tabernacle were fulfilled in the one sacrifice for Christ.

It may seem strange to prosaic minds to think of the heavenly things needing cleansing. However, the author was not drawing an exact parallel. In his method of interpretation he moved easily from the mundane to the spiritual sphere. And as Westcott notes, the heavenly cleansing was spiritual, not actual.

For Christ is not entered into the holy places made with hands, which are the figures [antetype, *antitupa*] **of the true; but into heaven itself, now to appear in the presence of God for us** (v.24).

The earthly **holy places** were the "counterpart of reality" (Moffatt). Christ has entered into **the true,** heaven itself, "now to appear before God for us" or "on our behalf" *(huper hemōn)*. Aaron appeared before God in his symbolic dwelling in mercy with Israel. But Christ has entered into the very presence of God.

Nor yet that he should offer himself often, as the high priest entereth into the holy place every year with blood of others (v.25).

Should offer is a present tense, to keep on offering. Christ does not need to do this as did Aaron, who annually did so bearing, not his own blood, but that of others or "belonging to another" (animals). The repetition and the kind of blood pointed toward fulfilment in a greater sacrifice.

For then must he often have suffered since the foundation of the world: but now once in the end of the world hath he appeared to put away sin by the sacrifice of himself (v.26).

Christ was the Lamb slain from the foundation of the world. In history this sacrifice was made to fulfil God's redemptive will. Had his sacrifice been no more efficacious than those made by Aaron, it would have been morally and spiritually necessary *(edei)* for him "to keep on suffering" *(pathein,* present infinitive) many times since the moment of creation.

But now changes from the supposition to the actual fact. The author could have hardly made the remainder of this verse stronger.

Once *(hapax),* once for all. **End of the world** means "consummation of the age." Christ's death marked the end of the old era and the beginning of the new. **Appeared** renders a perfect passive form of the verb *to manifest.* It was a full and final manifestation, and never to be repeated in sacrifice since none is necessary. His purpose was to put away or remove **sin** by the sacrifice of himself. Note the singular **sin.** The old covenant sacrifices dealt with individual transgressions. Jesus dealt with the sin-principle itself. He did this knowing that man faces a rendezvous with God.

And as it is appointed unto man once to die, but after this the judgment (v.27).

Man dies but once. But that is not the end. He must also face Christ as Judge. Now he is Saviour; then he will be Judge (cf. Matt. 25:31–46).

So Christ was once offered to bear the sins of many; but unto them that look for him shall he appear a second time without sin unto salvation (v.28).

In the Greek text there is a play on words: Once for all *(hapax)* Christ being offered (aorist participle of *prosphero)* to bear (aorist infinitive of *anaphero).* The two aorist tenses with "once for all" stress the *one* such act on the part of Christ. **Sins** should read "sin." Literally, "So also Christ, once for all being offered with respect to [*eis*] the sin of many to bear."

Moulton and Milligan comments on *anaphero* as used here more in the sense of *take away* (cf. Isa. 53:11). Christ is both the goat offering sacrificed on the altar and also the scapegoat bearing away the sin of men. This states both the fact and purpose of his death.

Corresponding to the idea of judgment in verse 27 is the Lord's return or his appearing a "second time." But this appearance will be **without** or "apart from" *(chōris)* sin **unto** [*eis*] **salvation.** *Eis* points to the goal of Jesus' redemptive work—salvation. **Salvation** here points to *glorification.* This will be for all the regenerated and sanctified ones. It includes the resurrection of the body (Rom. 8:23). In this passage in Romans, Paul speaks of the "redemption" of the body. The Greek word means "full-redemption" *(apolutrōsin tou sōmatos).* But glorification also involves the sum-total of glory and rewards in heaven. These shall be in proportion to the Christian's faithfulness in his state of sanctification.

Jesus came the first time to redeem from sin. He will come again to reward and glorify the redeemed. All Christians should be faithful in sharing the good news of redemption. So that those who receive it shall see the Lord's return as "the blessed hope" (Titus 2:13) and not as judgment unto eternal despair. The superior nature of Jesus' sacrifice makes the Christian's responsibility all the greater.

Notes

1. *Op. cit.*, p. 332.
2. *Op. cit.*, pp. 111 f., cf. Schneider, *op. cit.*, p. 82.
3. Robertson, *A Grammar of the Greek New Testament*, Doran, New York, 1923, p. 605.
4. *Op. cit.*, p. 148.
5. Moulton and Milligan, *op. cit.*, p. 630; cf. Hobbs, *Preaching Values from the Papyri*, Baker, Grand Rapids, 1964, pp. 118 ff.

X. The Historical Fulfilment

The author of Hebrews had shown the superiority of the new covenant over the old. After a summary statement he proceeded to show how God in Christ entered into history to effect his redemptive purpose. On this basis he again warned his readers against rebellion with respect to their own part in bringing the gospel of redemption to a lost world. He closed this part of his message by calling upon them to be faithful in their world-mission.

1. The Shadow of the True (10:1–4)

Previous references had been made to the sacrificial system under the old covenant as being but a type of its fulfilment in the new covenant. So here the author reiterated that fact, showing again why the former was unable to bring men into a right relation to God.

For the law having a shadow of good things to come, and not the very image of the things, can never with those sacrifices which they offer year by year continually make the comers thereunto perfect (v.1).

Coming first in the Greek text **shadow** is emphatic. It stands in contrast to **the image** (*eikona,* cf. "icon"). A shadow is made by an interruption of light, that interruption being made by the *image* itself. Coming events cast their shadows before them. So the coming of the *true* cast its shadow in the old covenant sacrifices.

Eikōn is used elsewhere of Christ being the exact manifestation of God (cf. 2 Cor. 4:4; Col. 1:15). So here Christ's sacrifice is seen as casting its shadow in the sacrifices of the old covenant. But as a shadow is not real, so were these sacrifices not the real work of God in redemption. They but pointed to it.

The plural **sacrifices** refers primarily to those annually *(kat' eniauton)* on the Day of Atonement. But they were also regarded as climaxing the sacrifices made throughout the year. Even though these were made **continually,** but not eternally, they were powerless to make the ones offering the sacrifices, priest and people, **perfect** (cf. 9:9). They failed to effect a right relation between God and men. For they were of law, not grace.

For then would they not have ceased to be offered? because that the worshippers once purged should have had no more conscience of sins (v.2).

The very repetition of these sacrifices proved their inefficacy. If they had effected a right relation between God and the worshipers, there would have been no need for further sacrifices. Having been cleansed of sins they would have had no **conscience** or "consciousness" of sins. It was their heart hunger which kept the priests and altars busy.

But in those sacrifices there is a remembrance again made of sins every year (v.3).

The old covenant system of sacrifice only reminded the people of their sins. It had no power to remove them. It convicted them, but could not cleanse them.

For·it is not possible that the blood of bulls and goats should take away sins (v.4).

Here **sins** should read "sin," the very principle of sin. **Take away** is a present infinitive, to keep on taking away sin. Or it could mean "from time to time to take away" sin as the blood of bulls and goats was taken into the Holy of Holies. It never at any time had done this. This very fact pointed away from the shadow to the **good things to come** (v.1). And on this basis the author turned to show how God had provided one whose sacrifice could take away sin.

2. The Fulness of the Time (10:5–10)

In Galatians 4:4–5 Paul spoke of the Incarnation of God in Jesus. He said, "But when the fulness of the time was come, God sent forth his Son, made of a woman, made under the law, to redeem them that were under the law." The author of Hebrews looked behind the scene, citing Psalm 40:6–8, to show the divine reasoning behind the Incarnation.

Wherefore when he cometh into the world, he saith, Sacrifice and offering thou wouldest not, but a body hast thou prepared me (v.5).

The author was quoting from the Septuagint. This is largely seen in his use of **body** rather than "ears."

Why did Christ enter into the arena of history? It was because animal sacrifices God *did not will* or *wish*. Such could not remove sin and effect a right relation between God and man.

The verb rendered **wouldest** is an aorist form second person singular. It pictures the Son speaking to the Father prior to the Incarnation. In eternity God had willed that only the sacrifice of a person, a divine Person, could provide the condition necessary for man's redemption. Hence, in essence, Jesus was the Lamb slain from the foundation of the world (cf. Rev. 13:8). This means that forgiveness was in the heart of God before sin was in the heart of man. For this reason God took the initiative in salvation. Since man could not be saved by law, God had willed a plan of redemption centered in grace. What the law could not provide, God provided through his Son.

Already it has been noted that man had to learn by experience that he could be saved by neither legalism nor by animal sacrifice. So in the fulness of time (when man had seen the inefficacy of these things), a time in God's own judgment or of his choosing, he sent forth his Son. Note the aorist form **prepared**. This may be viewed essentially as in God's will in eternity, and actually in Jesus' virgin birth. It should be noted also that **body** does not change the sense of Psalm 40:6. The "ears" are the part of the **body** through which God's will could be communicated.

In burnt offerings and sacrifices for sin thou hast no pleasure (v.6).

Sacrifices is not in the Greek text. However, one may see **burnt offerings** as inclusive of the entire sacrificial system of the old covenant. Actually the Greek text may read "burnt offerings and sin offering" *(peri hamartias)*. So in verses 5-6 the author mentions several offerings: animal sacrifice *(thusian)*, meal offering *(prosphoran)*, whole burnt offerings *(holokautōmata)*, and sin offering *(peri hamartias)*.

God had/has no pleasure in any of these as means of removing sin. So he **prepared** or "fitly framed" *(katērtisō)* a body for the Son that He might accomplish man's redemption.

However, this redemptive act involved not only the Father's but also the Son's will and work. This latter thought is expressed in verses 7-10.

Then said I, Lo, I come (in the volume of the book it is written of me,) to do thy will, O God (v.7; cf. Ps. 40:7-8).

The Son's will was submissive to the Father's will. Since the old covenant system could not suffice, the Son offered himself as the once-for-all sacrifice. The verb **come** *(hēkō)*, though a present tense, has the effect of a perfect tense (Arndt and Gingrich), so it means *fully come* or come as the fulfilment of the old covenant. As a religious term it refers to the coming of deity in a solemn appearance. This thought is emphasized in the use of **lo**. His purpose in coming was to do the Father's will (cf. v.5).

His coming had been prophesied **in the volume of the book**. **Volume** should read "roll." The word so rendered *(kephalidi)* is a diminutive form of *kephalē*, head.

It means a little head, but came to be used of a roll of writing. It appears only here in the New Testament, but is found in the papyri. **Is written** is a perfect tense of completeness. The Old Testament abundantly points to the coming of the suffering Servant of Jehovah (cf. Isa. 42:1—53:12).

Verses 8–9*a* repeat what is said above in verses 5–7. The old sacrifices centered in the law. The once-for-all sacrifice was the expression of God's grace.

He taketh away the first, that he may establish the second (v.9b).

The verb **taketh away** may also read "abolishes." Thus the old system of sacrifices (v.8) was abolished in the establishing of the new in the coming of Christ as Jesus of Nazareth.

By the which will we are sanctified through the offering of the body of Jesus Christ once for all (v.10).

The will of God was not fulfilled in animal sacrifice and other offerings (cf. vv. 4–6). But it was fulfilled in the once-for-all offering of the body of Jesus as an offering for sin. The superior High Priest offered himself as the *once-for-all (ephapax)* sacrifice, that through it he might provide for sinful men to be put into a right relation with God.

It was *in the sphere of (en)* this offering that the readers of this epistle, and all other Christians, **are sanctified.** Literally, "we have been sanctified" (periphrastic perfect passive indicative of *hagiazō,* to set apart). This expresses the thought previously stated. The believer is regenerated and set apart to God's service the moment that he receives Christ as Savior. Thereafter he is to develop and serve in that state of sanctification, looking toward his glorification in heaven at the Lord's return (cf. 9:28).

The old covenant sacrifices and offerings were designed to purify the Israelites that they might be qualified to worship and serve God. Since they were unable to accomplish this fully, Christ came to effect this relationship. The form of **are sanctified** shows that he did this fully as a finished work. Thus there is no reason why Christians should fail to be used of God in his work.

3. The Expectant Christ (10:11–18)

This section climaxes the author's contrast between the old and the new covenants. It reiterates the incompleteness of the old and explains the new.

And every priest standeth daily ministering and offering oftentimes the same sacrifices, which can never take away sins or "sin" (v.11).

Here is a vivid picture of the succession of priests "keeping on serving and keeping on offering according to the day [day after day] the same repeated sacrifices." The verb **standeth** is a perfect tense which emphasizes the fact that such services go on and on. The Levitical priests were never able *to sit down* (cf. v.12) or to cease their work. And yet their work never was able to remove utterly the sin of those for whom the service was rendered. It was not only a road that went on and on, but it also led to a desert of frustration. It was a dead-end street leading nowhere, had it not been for the sacrifice of Christ. It only pointed to the "good things to come" (cf. v.1).

But this man, after he had offered one sacrifice for sins for ever, sat down on the right hand of God; from henceforth expecting till his enemies be made his footstool (vv. 12–13).

With the adversative **but** the author turned from the Levitical ministry under the old covenant to Christ's ministry under the new. Almost every word in verse 12 may be contrasted with those of verse 11. "Every priest" versus **this man** (*houtos,* this one). "Offering oftentimes the same sacrifices" versus **offered one sacrifice . . . for ever.** "Offering" translates a present participle of repeated action. **Offered** renders an aorist participle of point action. **One** sacrifice as over against "oftentimes the same sacrifice." "Can never take away sin" versus **for** [*huper,* as a substitute, on behalf of] **sins.** "Standeth daily" [perfect tense] versus **sat down** (aorist). The priests continued their ministry; Christ rested from a completed ministry. He sits on the seat of power, rulership in his mediatorial kingdom (cf. 1 Cor. 15:25).

And what is he doing? He is **expecting** constantly. His redemptive work is behind him. From **henceforth** or with *respect to the rest* or *the future,* he is expecting "until his enemies be made his footstool." Here the author completed the cycle by citing Psalm 110:1 again (cf. 1:13). This is the promise and goal of Christ's redemptive work (cf. 1 Cor. 15:25 ff.).

This thought touches definitely upon the world-mission of God's people. Christ has finished his work in that mission. The rest depends upon his "holy brethren, partakers, [partners] of the heavenly calling" (cf. 3:1).

How these words in verse 13 should haunt every Christian! Christ is *expecting*. Expecting the Father to honor his promise to use his redemptive work redemptively. Just before he died on the cross Jesus said, "Father, into thy hands I commend my spirit" (Lk. 23:46). "Commend" renders a verb used in banking, to place on deposit (cf. 2 Tim. 1:12; "that which I have committed" reads, literally, "my deposit"). "Commend" or "commit" meant that one should safeguard the deposit and use it for its intended purpose. So Christ is expecting the Father to safeguard his redemptive work and use it for its intended purpose.

Furthermore, he is expecting his followers to proclaim his redemptive gospel. And that those who hear should heed and be saved thereby. Every time one soul submits to him another *enemy* becomes his footstool. And as Paul says in 1 Corinthians 15:25–28 Jesus looks to the time when he shall lay at the Father's feet a redeemed and subdued universe, both natural and spiritual, "that God may be all in all." God as Father, Son, and Holy Spirit; but God reigning supreme in his universe.

For by one offering he hath perfected for ever them that are sanctified (v.14).

This is why Jesus sat down and for the future is expecting. His one offering has done what all such under the old covenant could not do. **Perfected** is a perfect tense of *teleioō*. He has fully, completely finished the work of redemption whereby believers **are sanctified** or set apart to God's service. The present tense of this participle rendered "are sanctified," the ones being sanctified, could refer to a process working in the lives of believers. However, if one sees sanctification as a state achieved simultaneously with regeneration, the view of the writer, it may just as well read "the ones from time to time being sanctified" as they believe in Jesus.

The readers of this epistle had had such an experience. So here again is a reminder to them of their obligation to develop and serve in their state of being set apart unto God's service in his world-mission.

Whereof the Holy Ghost [Spirit] also is a witness to us (v.15).

This verse introduces the author's citation again of Jeremiah 31:31–34 (vv. 16–17; 8:8–12). This passage in Jeremiah had been inspired by the Holy Spirit. So in it he joined his witness to the will of the Father (v.5) and the work of the Son (v.7). This is a significant thing. In God's redemptive purpose the Father proposed redemption; the Son provided it: the Holy Spirit *propagates* it through the world-mission of God's people. As they are partners of the Son (3:1), so they are partners of the Holy Spirit (6:4) in this mission.

Now where remission of these is, there is no more offering for sin (v.18).

This refers to verse 17. This verse is the logical climax of the author's argument about the superior sacrifice offered by Christ (cf. 9:11—10:18). It fulfils Jeremiah's prophecy about the new covenant. And since Jesus' sacrifice has provided real remission concerning sin, there is no need for a further sacrifice.

It does not labor the point to note again the implication regarding the world-mission. There will be no other redemptive work of God in Christ. There is need for none. All that remains is that it be proclaimed to a lost world. And that is the work of the Lord's people in the power of the Holy Spirit. This is the essence of all the commissions given by Jesus after his resurrection (cf. Matt. 28:18–20; Luke 24:46–49; John 20:22–23; Acts 1:8). Yes, Jesus is expecting. Are his people working to bring to fruition that which he has done in providing redemption for all men (cf. John 15:1–8,16)?

4. The Fourth Exhortation (10:19–31)

This is the longest and sternest of the five exhortations. It is fitting that it should be, for it comes at the climax of the author's extended treatment of the superior nature of Christ's ministry over that under the old covenant. The readers' responsibility is proportionately greater. Failure brings a proportionately greater penalty. This exhortation consists of a basis (vv. 19–21), an encouragement (vv. 22–25), and a warning (vv. 26–31).

Having therefore, brethren, boldness to enter into the holiest by the blood of Jesus, by a new and living way, which he hath consecrated for us, through the veil, that is to say, his flesh; and having an high priest over the house of God (vv. 19–21).

The key word here is **boldness** as indeed it is one such throughout the epistle (cf. 3:6, 4:16; 10:19,35). Christians have boldness to enter into God's presence because of what Jesus has done. At his death the veil of the temple was torn asunder (cf. Matt. 27:51). Here the holy places are in heaven where Jesus has entered bearing his own blood (cf. 9:12). He continues to minister as High Priest over God's house as God's Son (cf. 3:6). So the Christian need be no stranger there, since he is Christ's brother and God's son.

Under the old covenant the high priest walked an old, oft-trodden way into the Holy of Holies. Even then it was unable to produce life. But Christ has provided **a new and living way. New** renders a word *(prosphaton)* which means "freshly killed." Christ's blood is powerful to save. It is not stale and dead. But to each one coming to him his blood is as though it had just been given for that one believer. It is a **living** way or one giving life.

The language here is highly symbolic. For instance, the **veil** here is not that barring one from God (cf. 6:20). The author points out that it is the flesh or the incarnation of Christ. It was through the incarnation that he became the entrance into the presence of God (cf. Jn. 14:6). So when the Christian comes without fear into God's presence, he finds a *Friend* there (v.21).

Because of this the author encouraged his readers to do three things. "Let us draw near." "Let us hold fast." "Let us consider one another." Each of these verbs is a present subjunctive. They are encouraged to keep on doing these things.

Let us draw near with a true heart in full assurance of faith, having our hearts sprinkled from an evil conscience, and our bodies washed with pure water (v.22).

A true heart in full assurance of faith suggests the opposite of 3:12. Rather than to rebel against God as did the Israelites at Kadesh-barnea, they should with pure hearts of obedient faith "come before" (actual meaning of draw near) him in worship and service. This could also refer to the people's fear as they stood apart from Mount Sinai when the old covenant was given. Under the new covenant of grace they are to come before God boldly to find grace to help in time of need—when they are tempted to rebel against his world-mission (cf. 4:15 f.).

They can do this because, like Aaron under the old covenant sprinkling animal blood, their hearts have been sprinkled with *Christ's blood*. And they have been cleansed with **pure water** as Aaron had cleansed his body. The perfect tense of **washed** means a thorough cleansing. Aaron had to repeat his cleansing annually on the Day of Atonement, but the Christian is permanently cleansed through Christ's atoning work.

Some see this as a reference to Christian baptism. However, the point here is cleansing of the body, not the soul. It makes better sense to see it as referring to Aaron's washing before entering the Holy of Holies with the blood to be sprinkled on the mercy seat (cf. Lev. 16:4,14).

Let us hold fast the profession of our faith without wavering; (for he is faithful that promised;) (v.23).

In the best Greek texts the word is "hope" rather than **faith.** Also "our" is not in the Greek text. So the confession is one characterized by hope. It is the guaranteed until the end hope spoken of in 3:6; 6:11,18; 7:19. Since it is a guaranteed hope, holding fast or having a firm grip on it does not refer to the possible loss of redemption. **Without wavering** suggests that the readers should not stand off from God in refusing to pursue the purpose of this confession of hope. Israel at Kadesh-barnea did not regard God as "faithful" or trustworthy in enabling her to achieve her place in his purpose for her as a priest-nation. The Hebrew Chrisians should not make the same mistake. God has promised better promises to them than to Israel (cf. 8:6), and they can trust him to keep them.

And let us consider one another to provoke unto love and good works: not forsaking the assembling of ourselves together, as the manner of some is; but exhorting one another: and so much the more, as ye see the day approaching (vv. 24–25).

These verses suggest mutual responsibility as these Christians face their common task. **Consider** means to put the mind down on one. They were to fix their minds or eyes on each other to avoid the danger of wavering in God's purpose. In doing so they should **provoke** (stimulate, incite) one another with respect to love and good works. They were to prop up each other in the cause of Christ.

They can serve this purpose by **not forsaking the assembling of ourselves together.** Some were falling victim to this. This is an exhortation to public worship in which all would be strengthened and encouraged in the Lord's work. One who never assembles for worship is hardly likely to be a good witness for Christ elsewhere. Thomas quotes Mackintosh to the effect that in the New Testament the word "saint" never occurs in the singular, and that "invariably it is plural." [1]

They were to be all the more faithful since **ye see the day approaching.** What day? The first thought probably would be the second coming of Christ (Robertson). Surely he taught his people to expect it at any time.

Since the author used **the day** he was thinking of some definite event. "The day" was often used in connection with Lord, Christ, and Son of man. "The day of the Lord" could refer to any great event in history which had religious significance. Westcott points out that the author's change to the direct address (*blepete,* see) adds force to the appeal. "The beginning of the Jewish war was already visible to the Hebrews." [2] Indeed, it most likely was in progress, even hastening to its terrible end (cf. 8:13). It would appear, therefore, that this is the day to which the author was referring. [3]

If so, it would mark a new day for the Christian cause. No longer would the world regard it as a branch of Judaism. So, opportunity was near to preach the gospel with new meaning and vigor, and the readers should be prepared to seize the opportunity. In times of difficulty God's people should be at their best. For it is in such times that people are most susceptible to the gospel message. It was against this background (vv. 19–25) that the author issued his warning.

For if we sin wilfully after that we have received the knowledge of the truth, there remaineth no more sacrifice for sins (v. 26).

Here again is one of the difficult passages in this epistle (vv. 26–31). Some see it as referring to apostasy or to the loss of redemption. However, in the light of previous and similar warnings the writer sees it as related to failure to fill one's place in God's world-mission. Again the author was drawing a lesson from events in the Exodus epic.

In the Greek text **wilfully** *(hekousiōs)* comes first, and so is emphatic. **Sin** translates a present participle. So the thought is that of wilfully keeping on sinning. Westcott points out two phases of such sin: Voluntariness in a conscience aware of the sin, and the habitual indulgence in it. [4]

The question is as to what sin the author had in mind. It was a sin which involved a "full-knowledge of the truth." Note "full-knowlege" *(epignōsis)* rather than "knowledge" *(gnōsis).* This suggests 6:4–5. Obviously the author regarded those committing this sin as being Christians. **The truth** is an absolute term and probably refers to God's full revelation in Jesus Christ (cf. John 14:6). So may not "full-knowledge" refer to this revelation as opposed to the partial one prior to Christ (cf. 1:1 ff.)? The old covenant was *gnōsis* about God. The new covenant was *epignōsis* through a personal experience with Jesus.

In 6:4 ff. the author spoke of rebellion against this covenant relationship. To do so was to rebel against God's redemptive purpose. It was noted earlier that Jesus' temptations were related to his place in that purpose (cf. 4:15 f.). So it is likely that the sin facing the Hebrew Christians was the same.

Therefore, the author said that if he and his readers should wilfully keep on sinning in rebellion against God's will for them in his world-mission (cf. 6:6), **there remaineth no more sacrifice for sins.** Christ made a once-for-all sacrifice in himself. It is all that is necessary for man's redemption. God has no plans for another redemptive act, and these Christians were not to delay waiting for it. Their responsibility was to proclaim the sacrifice already made.

Note that the sacrifice is for **sins.** Man is redeemed from *sin,* even as Israel was redeemed from Egyptian bondage. Subsequently the tabernacle sacrifices were designed to purify the people from sins that they might be fit for divine fellowship and service. Jesus redeemed from sin in his once-for-all sacrifice (1 Jn. 1:7). Thereafter his ministry in the heavenly tabernacle is to free his people from sins which violate their service relation to God (cf. 1 John 2:1).

Israel's repeated sins of provocation led to her rebellion at Kadesh-barnea. Even though she wanted to repent, she could not. So Christians who repeatedly and wilfully sin against their spiritual destiny, also will be deprived of their place in God's world-mission.

But a certain fearful looking for of judgment and fiery indignation, which shall devour the adversaries (v.27).

Rather than to expect God to provide another redemptive work or even cleansing from the sins of repeated rebellion, they can look for **judgment and fiery indignation** or a divine anger characterized by fire. Some interpreters would relate this verse to 2 Thessalonians 1:8–10. However, an examination of this passage will show that Paul was talking about the fate of unredeemed people. The author here was writing to redeemed people. Such fiery judgment will devour the **adversaries** or the ones standing opposite to God. This suggests the rebellion at Kadesh-barnea (cf. 3:12; 6:6). However, the author seems to have drawn this figure from another event in the Exodus epic.

He that despised Moses' law died without mercy under two or three witnesses (v.28). This statement apparently refers to Deuteronomy 17:2–7. The case there was of one who had broken the covenant with God by going into idolatry (v.2). Certainly such would negate his part in the covenant as a priest-nation. His life would not bring others to worship Jehovah. So at the mouth of two or three witnesses he should be stoned to death (v.6).

The focal point in the author's mind was such a person's *transgressing his covenant* or the covenant with God. So transposing this event to the author's words in Hebrews 10:28, sins of whatever kind would make his readers ineffective in God's world-mission. And such sins culminate in rebellion against it.

Of how much sorer punishment, suppose ye, shall he be thought worthy, who hath trodden under foot the Son of God, and hath counted the blood of the covenant, wherewith he was sanctified, an unholy thing, and hath done despite unto the Spirit of grace? (v.29). The author argued from the lesser to the greater. If such a sin as mentioned in Deuteronomy 17 brought death by stoning, certainly the sin mentioned here will bring a greater punishement.

Now for one who believes in apostasy this is a terrible but simple verse. But if one rejects that meaning what can be done with this statement? Certainly the author has moved from the Old Testament example to a New Testament application. But what was the possible sin facing his readers? It has been suggested as rebellion against the new covenant and the world-mission which it entails. The Old Testament context in Deuteronomy 17 supports this idea here.

Those who rebel against God's world-mission certainly tread under foot the Son of God. They hold him in contempt as the one who is the Saviour of the world. They join with his crucifiers in setting at naught his redemptive mission (cf. 6:6). Thus they count as unholy his blood which redeemed them and set them apart (sanctified) for their place in his redemptive mission. And they do despite to or insult the Holy Spirit of grace whose work is to be their divine partner (cf. 6:4) in this world-mission.

This is a terrible picture of those who receive redemption but refuse to be active in their state of sanctification in sharing the gospel with others. For such, a fate far worse than physical death is in store. They shall die in the wilderness of a lost opportunity. As stated before, to Christians in the flesh this may not seem so terrible. But when viewed in terms of eternal values it is terrible beyond description. Unhappily the world is filled with such Christians who are rebelling against God's will in evangelism and missions. Those who shame God by worshiping the things of the world certainly fall in this class. And those good-for-nothing Christians do the same.

For we know him that hath said, Vengeance belongeth unto me, I will recompense, saith the Lord. And again, The Lord shall judge his people (v. 30).

The author drove home his point by citing two passages from Deuteronomy (cf. 32:35 f.). These words came at the climax of Moses' final address, save his blessing (cf. Deut. 33), to the children of Israel. The Exodus epic was almost over, and he reminded them of their covenant as a priest-nation and how God would protect and use them. For the purpose of understanding Hebrews 10:30 it is necessary to examine Deuteronomy 32.

Moses began this address by calling upon heaven and earth to witness to God's redemptive purpose. "My doctrine shall drop as the rain, my speech shall distil as the dew, as the small rain upon the tender herb, and as the showers upon the grass: because I will publish the name of the Lord; ascribe ye greatness unto our God" (vv. 2–3). The chapter through verse 47 tells how Jehovah had prepared a people for his redemptive purpose, only to have them rebel against him. Subsequently they suffered at the hands of their enemies.

It is in this context that one may understand the author's words in Hebrews 10:30 (cf. Deut. 32:35 f.). However, the meaning is made clearer by referring to Deuteronomy 32:47. Moses concluded his address by saying, "For it is not a vain thing for you [to disregard your covenant relation]; because it is your life: and through this thing ye shall prolong your days in the land, whither ye go over Jordan to possess it."

Israel's covenant with Jehovah as a priest-nation was her reason for being, her very life as a nation. To rebel against it in Canaan was to invite trouble and sorrow. Ultimately this rebellion caused her to be set aside in favor of a people "which in time past were not a people, but are now the people of God" (1 Peter 2:10).

It was against this experience that the author of Hebrews warned his readers. For, like Israel, they would not be spared God's judgment if they rebelled against their new covenant. Missions and evangelism are the very life of any church or group of God's people. They are the reason for the being of God's people. He redeems them that he might use them.

God will judge his people; he will repay them in kind if they fail him. The wars and rumors of wars, all disturbances in today's world, are the fruit of the failure of the Lord's people to take seriously their place in God's world-mission. But even greater punishment is the loss of opportunity with its attendant blessings, both in this life and in that beyond this age.

It is a fearful thing to fall into the hands of the living God (v.31).

God is not dead but living. He is still seeking to lead his people to accept their place in his mission of world-redemption. He will not fail, but a rebellious generation of Christians, even one such Christian, can fail by *standing off* from God (cf. 3:12). And God does not take lightly such rebellion.

5. The Call to Faithfulness (10:32–39)

The author reminded his readers of their former faithfulness, and exhorted them to a renewed effort in God's purpose. He showed that they had not yet rebelled against God, and that he had hope that they would not do so.

But call to remembrance the former days, in which, after ye were illuminated, ye endured a great fight of afflictions; partly, whilst ye were made a gazingstock both by reproaches and afflictions; and partly, whilst ye became companions of them that were so used (vv. 32–33). **Call to remembrance** renders the present middle imperative of a verb, to remember or remind. It is a command to remind themselves of former experiences of faithfulness in the Lord's work. For **illuminated** see 6:4. This refers to their experience in becoming Christians. They had had to endure a conflict of many sufferings. They had been held up to derision, but had not been called upon to suffer violence (cf. 12:4). And they had shared in the sufferings of others.

For ye had compassion of me in my bonds, and took joyfully the spoiling of your goods, knowing in yourselves that ye have in heaven a better and an enduring substance (v. 34).

The best manuscripts read "the ones in bonds." It was not the author who had thus suffered, but other Christians, and the readers had suffered with them. Furthermore, they had accepted joyfully the plundering of their worldly possessions by those who persecuted them. For they knew that in heaven better and abiding possessions awaited them.

It is not stated where this took place. It was certainly true in Palestine and, doubtless, elsewhere. But they had endured, knowing that beyond the earthly sphere abundant and abiding reward awaited them in heaven. They should continue to be faithful with the same glorious expectation.

Cast not away therefore your confidence, which hath great recompence of reward (v.35). **Confidence** should read "boldness." The author exhorted them not to cast away as worthless their boldness in the faith. For they would receive reward in keeping with it. They should be bold not only to come to the throne of grace in time of need. They should also be bold to spread the gospel.

For ye have need of patience, that, after ye have done the will of God, ye might receive the promise. For yet a little while, and he that shall come will come, and will not tarry (vv. 36–37).

Patience is often regarded by modern men as simply waiting and enduring. But the Greek word *hupomonē* was a virile word. It was used of a soldier or athlete who could take all that the enemy or opponent could throw at him, yet have reserve strength with which to countercharge to victory. *Hupomonē* was used for a military citation.

So in their persecution these Hebrew Christians needed this quality, in order to fill their place in God's world-mission. This was to the end that having done God's will they would receive the **promise.** This was the very opposite to the Israelite rebellion at Kadesh-barnea. Doing God's will they would find that he not only could lead them into their "rest" (of Canaan) in which they were to carry out their mission (cf. 4:1). Also he could enable them to fulfil that mission in the work of their "sabbath-kind-of-rest" (cf. 4:9).

Verse 37*a* is a quotation of the Septuagint version of Isaiah 26:20. The latter part is from Habakkuk 2:3. The point is that the Coming One will soon appear to deliver and reward his people. *Ho Erchomenos,* the Coming One, was a designation for Christ. The promise here is that they should be faithful in their mission for the Lord, looking for the return of Christ. That he has not yet returned does not mean that the author was in error. Jesus had told his people to look for his return at any moment. Such an expectation should hold God's people to the task of evangelism in every age.

Now the just shall live by faith: but if any man draw back, my soul shall have no pleasure in him (v.38).

The opening part of this verse is a quotation of Habakkuk 2:4*b*. The latter part is from Habakkuk 2:4*a* (Septuagint). For his purpose the author transposed the verse. It is the only verse from the Old Testament that is quoted three times in the New Testament (cf. Rom. 1:17; Gal. 3:11). In these cited passages Paul used it to show that one is saved by faith and not by works.

But there is one difference between Hebrews 10:38 and the other two New Testament usages. For here the author used *mou,* of me, my, after "the just." It may properly read "My righteous [justified] one out of faith shall live." The meaning is that a Christian shall live out of (find his source for living) faith. So the sense in Hebrews 10:38 seems to be that a redeemed man shall live his Christian life in strength growing out of faith. It is the faith which enables one to fulfil God's purpose for his life (cf. Heb. 11). This also suggests the lack of faith on Israel's part at Kadesh-barnea.

If any man shall draw back from duty through *no faith* (cf. 3:12), God will not be pleased with him. He shall suffer the punishment of God for unfaithfulness.

But we are not of them who draw back unto perdition: but of them that believe to the saving of the soul (v.39).

But we is emphatic, in contrast to those who because of no faith draw back from their Christian duty (cf. 3:12; 6:6). The word **perdition** (*apōleian,* cf. Apollyon) here carries not the modern idea of hell, but that of its basic sense of destruction. This was the fate of the Israelites who shrank back at Kadesh-barnea. They lost their opportunity and their lives.

The author saw his readers as not repeating the rebellion at Kadesh-barnea. Instead they were the ones having faith that God can lead them to achieve their spiritual destiny in his redemptive mission.

The word rendered **saving** (*peripoiēsin* from *peripoieō*) means a working around or *preserving*. It does not mean *saving* in the usual gospel connotation.[5] This sense of *preserving* is strengthened in its use with "soul" *(psuchē)*. This word sometimes was used in classical Greek and in Philo for "life." In both, the exact phrase found here is used in the sense of saving one's life. The word might be used for either "life" or "soul" (cf. Matt. 16:25 f.).

The sense in Hebrews 10:39 seems to be "life" or the very purpose for one's being. In the case of these Hebrew Christians that was their world-mission. Their *souls* had been saved through regeneration. And their *lives* had been sanctified or set apart unto God's service. Through faithful performance in their mission for God they would save or preserve the very purpose of their being. And thus they could look forward to glorification at the Lord's return (cf. v.37).

Notes

1. *Op. cit.,* p. 134.
2. *Op. cit.,* p. 328.
3. See Thomas, *op. cit.,* p. 134.
4. *Op. cit.,* p. 330.
5. Cf. Thomas, *op. cit.,* p. 139

XI. The Roll Call of the Faithful

This chapter should not be read in isolation. Thomas suggests that 10:22–25 exhorts toward faith, hope, and love. These virtues are enlarged upon in the three final chapters respectively.[1]

Chapter 11 is an enlargement upon 10:38–39. The author showed how others of God's people had found in faith a source of strength to enable them to fulfil their God-given purpose in their lives. And upon this basis he exhorted his readers to be faithful in their part in God's plan and purpose.

1. The Practical Value of Faith (11:1-3)

Faith is one of the key words in Hebrews. The verb *pisteuō* is found only in 4:3; 11:6. But the substantive *pistis* (faith) is used thirty-two times, twenty-four times in Chapter 11. It is the opposite of the *no faith* mentioned in 3:12, 19. So whereas Israel at Kadesh-barnea had rebelled due to a lack of faith, those mentioned in this chapter had lived victoriously "by faith" or with faith as the instrument. It should be remembered that "faith" in Chapter 11 is not the faith by which one is redeemed but faith by which to live a full and effective life in the will of God.

Now faith is the substance of things hoped for, the evidence of things not seen (v.1). The author was not defining faith but expressing characteristics about it. He was preparing to illustrate his argument that it is through faith that one finds strength to live within God's will.

In this verse there are two parallels: *substance* and *evidence; things hoped for* and *things not seen.* Faith deals with the future, with things as yet unrealized in experience. *Things seen* are no longer in the realm of probability. They are facts of experience. And when hope has been fulfilled, it is no longer in the future but in the past and present.

It is faith which sees the reality in things yet in the future. It is the evidence and the proof. **Substance** renders a word meaning something placed under an object to give it firmness and support, such as a building, promise, or contract. Moulton and Milligan translate Hebrews 11:1, "Faith is the *title-deed* of things hoped for." [2] **Evidence** may be read as "proof" or "conviction." After something is proved it becomes a conviction. "Conviction" probably should be seen here, but either makes sense.

Thus, faith is basic in every area of life. It is the support which stabilizes every element of society. Even scientific research begins with faith that truth not yet known can be discovered. Certainly faith is a vital element in one's spiritual life. When reason falters faith can lead one on to great achievements. It can bridge the chasm between what is and what can be. The readers of this epistle, then and now, need this title-deed and conviction.

For by it the elders obtained a good report (v.2). **Elders** refers to all the faithful who had preceded the readers of this epistle. It is used more in the sense of "fathers," the forefathers in the faith. **Obtained a good report** should read "were testified to" or "had witness borne to" or "of" them. Living by faith their lives were witnessed to as victorious in God's eternal purpose.

Through faith we understand that the worlds were framed by the word of God, so that things which are seen were not made of things which do appear (v.3).

Obviously such a tremendous truth must be understood by faith. No man was there when God by his spoken word created "the ages." The things visible to the eye did not come into being through any eternally existing matter. Thus the author denies the eternity of matter, and affirms that the universe was created by the spoken word of God (cf. Gen. 1:3; John 1:1–3; Col. 1:16; Heb. 1:2).

So in three brief verses the author set the stage for his roll call of the faithful. As faith was the *title-deed* and *conviction* of the elders, both looking back to the beginning and looking forward to the future, so should the readers perform by faith the work designed of God for them.

2. The Antediluvian Faith (11:4–7)

This antediluvian division was not necessarily in the author's mind. But it forms a natural grouping leading up to Abraham. The point is that each of these men exercised faith in a given situation, and that God blessed them in it.

By faith Abel offered unto God a more excellent sacrifice than Cain, by which he obtained witness that he was righteous, God testifying of his gifts: and by it he being dead yet speaketh (v.4).

This is the faith of *worship*. Why Abel's sacrifice was more abundant or excellent than Cain's is not stated in Genesis 4:4. Some see the difference in the offering itself. Cain offered the fruit of the field; Abel's offering involved the death of a victim. Others see it in the quantity of the offerings. Perhaps the difference lay in the spirit in which the offerings were made.

This seems to be the point in verse 4. Abel offered **by faith.** Since this was the first recorded act of worship, perhaps God had revealed his will for it. And Abel by faith responded properly to the revelation. Thus he had it witnessed to himself as being **righteous** or as corresponding to the will of God. God gave witness to his gifts as being within his will. And through it, through his faith, Abel having died keeps on speaking. He continues through the ages to witness to the fact that God honors faith in his word.

By faith Enoch was translated that he should not see death; and was not found, because God translated him: for before his translation he had this testimony,

that he pleased God (v.5).

This was the faith of *fellowship*. The reference is to Genesis 5:24. "Enoch walked with God." This implies faith, friendship, harmony, love, obedience, trust, and mutual understanding. Life with God on earth was so natural that God took him to himself without the experience of death. The basis of Enoch's translation was his faith. It was before his translation that he had the testimony that he was well-pleasing to God. The perfect tense shows how completely this was true.

But without faith it is impossible to please him; for he that cometh to God must believe that he is, and that he is a rewarder of them that diligently seek him (v.6). Some see this verse as an interlude in the discussion. In a sense this is true. But it also further explains verse 5. **Impossible** (cf. 6:4,18) is a strong word. Apart from faith it is impossible to be well-pleasing to God or to be in fellowship with him.

Everyone who approaches God as a worshiper must believe in his existence and that he is active both morally and spiritually. God responds to faith in the revelation of himself. And anyone who seeks him, literally, seeks him out, will be rewarded by finding him. The Russian cosmonaut said that in space he saw God nowhere. The American astronaut said that in space he saw God everywhere.

By faith Noah, being warned of God of things not seen as yet, moved with fear, prepared an ark to the saving of his house; by the which he condemned the world, and became heir of the righteousness which is by faith (v.7).

This was the faith of *obedience*. "Being warned" refers to a divine communication (cf. Gen. 6:13 ff.). Though the flood was one hundred and twenty years in the future Noah believed God's word. And he acted upon it. **Moved with fear,** "godly fear" or "reverence," he built an ark according to God's specifications. It took quite a lot of faith to do this in a land where such seemed useless. And in the face of ridicule by evil men. But his faith was rewarded threefold: he saved his family; he judged unto condemnation the unbelieving world; he became heir to the "according to faith righteousness" (cf. Rom. 1:17). Noah is also called "a preacher of righteousness" (2 Peter 2:5), and all because of his faith.

Here then were three men in the dawn of God's revelation who by faith achieved in keeping with God's purpose. And they became living testimonies that God's justified ones shall live by faith (cf. 10:38).

3. The Faith of the Patriarchs (11:8–22)

The first three examples of faith spanned the vast reaches of time from the creation up to what may be called history in the sense of that which touches upon events of history in the commonly accepted use of the word. The others were no less historical. But beginning with Abraham one is within the context of history which submits to the records of nations.

By faith Abraham, when he was called to go out into a place which he should after receive for an inheritance, obeyed; and he went out, not knowing whither

he went (v.8). This was the faith of *adventure.* Verses 8–22 relate to the Genesis record beginning with 11:31. The specific verses in mind here are Genesis 12:1–5. Beginning with Hebrews 11:8 the author touched definitely upon God's redemptive purpose. For it was in Abraham that God chose a man through whose line it would run. Here the author chose his primary example of faith. Paul spoke of him as "faithful Abraham" (Gal. 3:9).

Abraham's faith is seen in his willingness to leave the well-established life of Ur of the Chaldees to venture out on God's word. He left home, family, and friends to become a wanderer in the earth. He left the *seen* for the *unseen.* He believed God's promise of an inheritance when there was no tangible evidence regarding it. Truly his faith was his *title-deed* to a land about which he knew nothing. **Knowing** renders a present middle participle of *epistamai,* to put the mind on something. When he went out he had not the slightest idea where he was going. He walked by faith when he could not walk by sight. Every step that he took was one into the unknown. But he took each one **by faith.**

By faith he sojourned in the land of promise, as in a strange country, dwelling in tabernacles with Isaac and Jacob, the heirs with him of the same promise: for he looked for a city which hath foundations, whose builder and maker is God (vv. 9–10).

The verb **sojourned** *(paroikeō)* is related to the substantive *paroikos* (cf. Acts 7:6) which was used for a foreigner who was a licensed sojourner. He became a resident-alien by paying a small tax for the privilege of living in a country short of citizenship that he might live and do business in the land. Such a person was Abraham in the very land that God had promised to give him. A man of lesser faith would have fretted at such, wondering why God did not hasten to fulfil his word. The land of promise was **as in a strange country** *(allotrian)* or a land not his own. The word meant "belonging to another."

Whereas in Ur he probably had lived in a house, in Canaan he lived in tents. Tents were temporary, insecure dwellings, whose only security was pegs driven into the ground. It was the life of a nomad.

He did this by faith, for he **looked** for "the city" having foundations. Note the contrast between nomadic dwelling and "the city," a definite city. Also the contrast between tent pegs driven into the ground and "the of the foundations having city." Robertson speaks of "looked for" as the steady and patient waiting in spite of disappointments.

The figure of "the city" suggests heaven. Abraham was a resident alien on earth, but he by faith looked beyond the *now* to the *then.* One does not do violence to this in seeing also the complete fulfilment of God's promise to Abraham and his seed. For the goal of such was a redeemed people in a redeemed universe provided by Christ, the true seed of Abraham (cf. Gal. 3:16). All of this embodied God's redemptive purpose.

Through faith also Sara herself received strength to conceive seed, and was delivered of a child when she was past age, because she judged him faithful who had promised (v.11). This is faith in the midst of *frustration.* Sarah is mentioned here because of her oneness with Abraham, and whose faith was a condition for the fruition of his faith (Westcott).

The story is one of frustration and doubt. Though Sarah was past the age for normal childbearing, God had promised Abraham and Sarah a son through whom God's promise should run. Despairing of such, Sarah arranged for her husband, in keeping with the custom of the time, to have a son by her servant Hagar (cf. Gen. 16). Still God promised a son by Sarah (cf. Gen. 17:16 ff.). Later Sarah laughed in unbelief at the idea (cf. Gen. 18:12 ff.). But God assured Abraham that nothing was too hard for Him to do (v.14) and in due time Isaac was born.

In his example of Abraham's faith Paul centered it in this experience (Rom. 4:18–22). "Who against hope believed in hope . . . and being yet weak in faith . . . he staggered not at the promise of God through unbelief; but was strong in faith, giving glory to God."

There sprang there even of one, and him as good as dead, so many as the stars of the sky in multitude, and as the sand which is by the sea shore innumerable (v.12).

Though his aged body was as good as dead insofar as natural conception was concerned, by his faith he learned that God was trustworthy to fulfil his promise (cf. Gen. 22:17). Some question the virgin birth of Jesus, but scarcely mention the births of Isaac and John the Baptist. Though not virgin born they were born supernaturally. Like Mary, Abraham and Sarah learned that "not shall be impossible alongside God any word" (Luke 1:37). What God says, God can perform, and Abraham and Sarah found it to be true.

These all died in faith, not having received the promises, but having seen them afar off, and were persuaded of them, and embraced them, and confessed that they were strangers and pilgrims on the earth. For they that say such things declare plainly that they seek a country (vv. 13–14).

And were persuaded is not in the best texts. The reference here is inclusive of all of Abraham's immediate descendants. They did not live to see the promises fulfilled. But they held on to them in faith or "according to faith" *(kata pistin)*. They lived in the sphere of faith and their characters were made sturdy in faith. They saw the fulfilment of their faith afar off. But they **embraced** or greeted it as a reality. Abraham did not live to see the Messiah personally, but by faith he saw His day and rejoiced (cf. John 8:56).

In faith they confessed that they were **strangers** (*xenoi,* foreigners) and **pilgrims** *(parepidēmoi)* on the earth. *Parepidēmos* was used for a foreigner who was just passing through a land. He might take up temporary residence in an alien land, but did not become a part of its life (cf. 1 Peter 1:1; 2:11). By faith they were pilgrims in the earth, but their citizenship was in heaven (cf. v.10). And like Abraham, a resident alien, they were there on business for their King.

The language of living on the part of the patriarchs demonstrated that they were living in an *allotrian,* a country belonging to another (cf. v.9). And that they were seeking a *patrida,* a country of their own. They were not to obtain it by conquest but as a gift of God's grace (cf. v.10).

And truly, if they had been mindful of that country from whence they came out, they might have had opportunity to return. But now they desire a better country, that is, an heavenly: wherefore God is not ashamed to be called their God: for he hath prepared for them a city (vv. 15–16). The author was still talking about the patriarchs. But by inference one may see also the attitude of Israel at Kadesh-barnea. The latter had considered returning to the bondage of Egypt. But were not permitted to do so.

However, had the patriarchs been mindful of Ur of the Chaldees, they might have had opportunity to return there. The verb rendered **had been mindful** is an imperfect tense meaning to remember, a continuing action in past time. It could mean to be homesick. But in the light of verse 14 it may be seen in the sense of making mention of Ur, in other words, had their talking been about Ur rather than their spiritual destiny: **Have had** also renders an imperfect tense. They would have kept on having an opportune time to return to Ur.

It should be recalled, however, that they were in Canaan on the basis of faith in God's promise. Israel had promises, but they were to a *redeemed* nation under a covenant of service. She was held back from returning to Egypt by her covenant agreement with God. She dishonored the agreement and lost her opportunity. The patriarchs were in Canaan purely on faith. They could have returned to Ur. But the result would have been the same as that of Israel's rebellion. God's redemptive purpose would have been delayed but not defeated, and the patriarchs would have lost their opportunity in it.

But now introduces the real attitude of the patriarchs. **Desire** means to stretch out or yearn after something. The present tense expresses a continuous state. Their hearts were fixed upon God's spiritual purpose for them. And though they did not live to see its fulfilment, they had faith to believe in its ultimate accomplishment. For this reason Jehovah was not ashamed to be called their God, "the Lord God of your fathers, the God of Abraham . . . Isaac, and . . . Jacob" (Ex. 3:15). He had prepared for them a city. Westcott comments,

The proof of God's acceptance of the patriarchs lies in what He did for them. Their faith truly corresponded with His purpose. They entered into His design and He acknowledged their devotion and trust. He was pleased to establish a personal relation with them, and to fulfil His spiritual promise; for "He prepared for them a city." He made provisions for their abiding continuance with Him in the fulness of human life. The statement is made in the most absolute form without any definition of time.[3]

By faith Abraham, when he was tried, offered up Isaac; and he that had received the promises offered up his only begotten son, of whom it was said, That in Isaac shall thy seed be called: accounting that God was able to raise him up, even from the dead; from whence also he received him in a figure (vv. 17–19). This was the faith of *supreme trial.* Surely this was the greatest of all the tests of Abraham's faith. The word rendered **was tried** is a present passive participle of the verb to test *(peirazō).* It was also rendered as "tempt" (cf. Gen. 22:1, KJV).

The sense in this cited passage is that of a testing. Satan tempts or tests men to prove them false. God puts men to the test, or permits such, to prove them genuine (cf. Job's testings). This latter is the sense in Hebrews 11:17.

Abraham lived in an environment where pagan people did sacrifice their children to their gods. Did Abraham love Jehovah as much as they loved their idols? Would he trust God to keep his promise through Isaac even though the boy should die? A reading of the Genesis account shows how great was the test of a father's love and of his faith in God. The present participle of *peirazō* shows the continuing testimony of the patriarch's faith.

By faith Abraham **offered up** Isaac. The perfect tense shows that in his heart he had already sacrificed Isaac before God stayed his hand. It was something like God the Father in eternity having given his only begotten Son in sacrifice. But unlike Abraham's case, he did not provide a ram as a substitute at Calvary.

Abraham did this **accounting** what God could do in order to fulfil his promise (v.19). God had promised that his purpose should be through Isaac. Now he told Abraham to sacrifice him. So the father did some calculating. He concluded that somehow God would keep his promise. Even if he had to raise Isaac from the dead. If God in the first place could give Isaac to him in a miraculous birth, he was able also to give him back to him in a miraculous raising from the dead. It was in this assurance of faith that Abraham obeyed God's command.

The author said that Abraham's experience with Isaac was a **figure** or parable (*parabolē*, cf. 9:9). The word is used in the sense of a *type*. The entire incident is a type of God giving his Son to die and then raising him from the dead that he might carry out his redemptive purpose. Nothing, not even death of the seed of Abraham (cf. Gal. 3:16), could prevent God from fulfilling his purpose. Indeed, it was the means by which he made it possible.

Verses 20–22 simply add to the abiding faith of the patriarchs. They followed the example of Abraham in believing God's promise regardless of the circumstances under which they lived. It is ever "by faith" on the part of God's people that his redemptive purpose has found fruition in the annals of history.

4. The Faith of Moses (11:23–29)

In these verses the author moved to the next stage in the implementing of God's redemptive purpose. It was through Moses that God prepared a people to be a priest-nation in that purpose.

By faith Moses, when he was born, was hid three months of his parents, because they saw he was a proper child; and they were not afraid of the king's commandment (v.23).

This was the faith of *daring love*. It is based upon Exodus 2:2. The faith described here was that of his parents. Pharaoh had ordered all male babies born to the Israelites to be thrown into the river. He was trying to curb the rapid growth of this enslaved people. When Moses was born, his parents saw that he was a "proper" or "goodly" child. Evidently something about him led his parents to believe that he was to fill a special role in the plans of God. This conviction relieved them of fear as to what the ruler might do. They feared God more than they feared the king. So they hid the baby for three months.

Exodus 2:3 ff. tells how Moses was spared and eventually came to be a part of the royal household. Only thus could he have been spared and reared to fill his later role in God's purpose.

By faith Moses, when he was come to years, refused to be called the son of Pharaoh's daughter; choosing rather to suffer affliction with the people of God, than to enjoy the pleasures of sin for a season; esteeming the reproach of Christ greater riches than the treasures in Egypt: for he had respect unto the recompense of the reward (vv. 24–26).

This is the faith of *self-denial* (cf. Ex. 2:11 ff.). Moses made a deliberate choice in renouncing his royal status to identify himself with his suffering people. The word translated **choosing** means that he had to take a definite position. He could have gone on enjoying the sinful pleasures of the royal court for a time. But at death he would have left behind a wasted life. Instead he took the position of suffering evil with his own people, the people of God. Had he not done so, he would soon have been forgotten. Because of his temporary self-denial, he towers as one of the giants of history.

Moses struck a balance of values in life. It showed that the reproach of Christ was greater riches than all of the perishable treasures of an empire. He **had respect** to or kept on looking away from worldly gain and glory to the reward of God's people in heaven (cf. Matt. 6:19 ff.).

Since the author mentioned Christ one wonders as to his meaning. Had Moses' mother planted the seed of a messianic hope in his heart (cf. Deut. 18:15)? This is not necessarily the meaning. Perhaps the author was saying that as Christ suffered reproach to be man's Redeemer, so Moses also chose to suffer at men's hands in order to fulfil God's purpose for him. As one reads Exodus this idea is not clearly spelled out. But it was involved in the purpose of God as he worked through events to raise up a leader for his people.

By faith he forsook Egypt, not fearing the wrath of the king: for he endured, as seeing him who is invisible (v.27). This is the faith of *deliberate choice* (cf. Ex. 2:15). The Exodus account says that he fled before the ruler's purpose to kill him. But the author saw through the event of the moment to God's ultimate purpose. God worked in current events to lead his servant into Midian where he would be prepared for his life's work.

So Moses' fleeing was not in fear of man. It was following a conviction not yet clear to him but which in time God made plain. He saw by faith what could not be seen by the natural eye. This must be the case of anyone who assays to work for God.

Through faith he kept the passover, and the sprinkling of blood, lest he that destroyed the firstborn should touch them (v.28). This was the faith of *submission* (cf. Ex. 12:1 ff.). God was ready by a mighty hand to deliver his people. By this time Moses had so lived with and wrought for God, that his disposition was to obey God's every word. He did not ask why the passover lamb should be killed and its blood sprinkled on the doorposts. He simply did what God said.

God honored his promise. Because Moses and the people submitted themselves unto God, he did what only God could do. The passover became the greatest of all the Jewish feasts. It reminded them that through their submissive faith God could deliver them from cruel bondage. And it pointed to him who is the Lamb of God delivering from the bondage of sin all who receive him.

By faith they passed through the Red sea as by dry ground: which the Egyptians assaying to do were drowned (v.29).

This is faith in *God's word* (cf. Ex. 15:5 ff.). With the foreboding waters before them Moses and the Israelites had only God's word that they could cross over safely. They did not question but marched across on dry ground. The very walls of water which at God's word protected them, engulfed and destroyed the Egyptian army.

When God says, "Go forward," men may see many obstacles. But if they start walking God will open the way. This is parallel in thought to Israel at Kadesh-barnea but with different results.

It is significant that the author used more examples from Moses than anyone else. Could this be that he was thinking about the Exodus epic? To be sure he made no further mention of it except Israel's entrance into Canaan (vv. 30 f.). But the idea is interesting nevertheless.

Thomas summarizes the faith of Moses in an interesting way:

The faith of Moses calls for special attention from all who live the life of trust. We see three things: (a) Faith's vision. Moses saw through temporal things and penetrated to eternal realities because he saw God (v.27). (b) Faith's value. Moses chose, reckoned, separated himself, and determined to do the will of God. (c) Faith's victory. He overcame the world as represented by Egypt, the opposition of Pharaoh, and the power of his own natural tendencies as he was tempted by the glories of Egypt.[4]

5. The Summary of the Faithful (11:30–38)

Following his treatment of Moses the author made brief reference to the faith of Joshua and the Israelites and of Rahab (vv. 30 f.). The number was too great to cite in the alloted space. He mentioned in one sentence such worthies as Gideon, Barak, Samson, Jephthae, David, Samuel, and the prophets (v.32). Then he listed anonymously a host of heroes of faith (vv. 33–38). One can by examination discover some of these. The events extend from the period of Judges to the time of the Maccabees. **Subdued kingdoms** could include all those listed in verse 32. Josephus used this idea for David's conquests. David, the great king, and Samuel, the statesman-prophet epitomize all that is noble in the nation's history. All of Israel's righteous history was viewed as in the purpose of Jehovah.

Stopped the mouths of lions, quenched the violence of fire obviously refers to Daniel in the lion's den and to the three Hebrews in the fiery furnace (cf. Dan. 6:18–23; 3:19–28). The Old Testament is filled with instances which could fit the remainder of verse 34. The women receiving their dead raised to life again certainly suggest 1 Kings 17:17 ff.; 2 Kings 4:17 ff.

Others were tortured, not accepting deliverance; that they might obtain a better resurrection (v.35).

This is a reference to a non-biblical event during the Maccabean period (cf. 2 Maccabees 6:18 ff.; 7). Rather than to deny their faith in Jehovah to espouse Greek pagan gods, a mother saw her seven sons dismembered and fried. All the while she exhorted them not to deny God, saying that he would raise them from the dead.

Others like Zechariah, were stoned to death (v.37, cf. 2 Chron. 24:20). This was the customary Hebrew form of capital punishment. **Sawn asunder,** according to tradition, was Isaiah's form of death (cf. 2 Sam. 12:31; 1 Chron. 20:3).

Going about in sheepskins and goatskins suggests prophets, like Elijah and Elisha. *Mēlōtē* was used in the Septuagint for the prophets' dress (cf. 1 Kings 19:13,19; 2 Kings 2:8,13–14). **Of whom the world was not worthy (v.38).** Though they were rejected by the world, they were of more value than it all. **Worthy** *(axios)* has the idea of scales. Put the prophets on one side and the world on the other, and the former far outweighs the latter.

Thus the author concluded his list of the faithful. They achieved each in his own God-given responsibility through faith. They *believed* in God. They *trusted* in God. And they *committed* themselves to God. All of these things are bound up in the word "faith." The obvious lesson is that the readers of this epistle, then and now, should follow their example. Indeed they must if they are to achieve for God in their own sphere of responsibility.

6. The Present Role of the Faithful (11:39–40)

It was in these verses that the author drew his conclusion with respect to his readers. He likens God's redemptive world-mission to a relay race (cf. 12:1 ff.).

And these all, having obtained a good report through faith, received not the promise (v.39).

These all includes the entire group in verses 4–38. They were witnessed to as being faithful. Yet they did not live to see the final fulfilment of the promise. They did receive promises as may be seen in their own achievements. But **the promise** refers to a definite one, the messianic promise. Abraham in faith saw Messiah's day and rejoiced. Moses by faith suffered reproaches as did Christ. But no one of these Old Testament or interbiblical worthies lived to see the Christ and his redemptive work.

God having provided some better thing for us, that they without us should not be made perfect (v.40).

Having provided should read "foresaw" (aorist of *problepō*, to see before). He foresaw "something better," the better promises (cf. 8:6) for the author and his readers. They had lived to experience the redemptive work of Christ in their own lives *by faith* in him.

But that was not all. **In order that not apart from us they should be made perfect. Be made perfect** renders *teleioō*, to bring something to its intended goal.

Here then is the author's purpose in leading his readers through this Westminster Abbey of faith. It was to challenge them to a like faith in God's world-mission.

Keep in mind the idea of a relay race. Suppose that every man save the last one runs faithfully and wins his segment of the race. If the last man fails, then all have lost the race. Insofar as the overall race is concerned they might just as well have not run victoriously. The ultimate victory depends upon the final runner.

Those who went before the readers had won their segments of the race. But if these Hebrew Christians did not run their part of the race, then the race would be lost. Of course, God would find another people to carry out his purpose. But like Israel at Kadesh-barnea, the purpose would be delayed. For those who went before to see the overall purpose accomplished or completed, every generation of Christians must *by faith* win its segment of the race.

Almost two thousand years have elapsed since Jesus wrought his redemptive work. How long would it take for the human race to go back to stark paganism? Just one generation of Christians who fail to preach the gospel. It is no wonder then why the author exhorted his readers to faithfulness. It is understandable why God gave the severe warnings through him.

Christian people have a better covenant based upon better promises. They have a message based upon the true, not on the shadow. It is incumbent upon them, therefore, by faith to achieve in their segment of God's eternal mission of redemption as their forefathers in the faith did in theirs.

Notes

1. *Op. cit.,* p. 140
2. *Op. cit.,* p. 660.
3. *Op. cit.,* p. 366; cf. Schneider, *op. cit.,* p. 109; Grant, *op. cit.,* p. 52.
4. *Op. cit.,* pp. 150 f.

XII. The Call to a World Mission

The author had finished his argument. So he drew his conclusion. The chapter division is unfortunate here. For 12:1–3 really is the climax of Hebrews 11. But even so the sense is preserved. For after exhorting his readers the author went on to show how they should go on to victory in spite of their present trials. While the application of chapter 11 is seen in 12:1–3, the entire chapter is an exhortation to Christian duty. It is a call to a world-mission.

1. The Fifth Exhortation (12:1–3)

This exhortation is different from the others in that it contains no warning, but see verses 25–29. In verses 1–3 the author appealed to the highest motives growing out of the examples of faith cited in chapter 11. Westcott outlines these verses as follows: (a) the position, (b) the preparation, (c) the effort, (d) the aim, of Christians looking to One who had himself conquered through suffering. The position is that of a great arena. The preparation involves the readers' getting ready to run the race. The effort is the manner of running. And the aim is to be victorious for Jesus' sake.

Wherefore seeing we also are compassed about with so great a cloud of witnesses, let us lay aside every weight, and the sin which doth so easily beset us, and let us run with patience the race that is set before us (v.1).

Wherefore introduces a conclusion of emphasis. It may refer immediately to the faithful in Hebrews 11. But in the larger sense it includes everything in the epistle up to this point. Because they have a better revelation, ministry, and sacrifice in Christ, the new covenant over the old, they are exhorted to faithfulness even beyond that of the heroes of chapter 11.

"We also" points to the author and readers as over against the heroes of faith in their past history. The author sees the present generation of God's people as being **compassed about with so great a cloud of witnesses.** The figure is that of a stadium with tier upon tier of people sitting in the stands. They are "lying around us" as a cloud hovering over the landscape.

This **cloud** is composed of **witnesses** *(marturōn).* They are not simply spectators *(theatōn)* watching the race. They are that to be sure. But they are more. They are the *heroes* who have had witness borne to their faithfulness (cf. 11:2,39). They have witnessed to the fact that by faith one can be true to God and can accomplish his purpose. Having won their own victories, they have sat down in the stadium to see how the present generation will fare. Thus they are keenly interested in the outcome because the ultimate victory of which theirs were parts depends upon the present runners. To present-day Christians this cloud of witnesses has been enhanced by all who have wrought victoriously since the author wrote these words.

In this position the present runners were to make certain preparations. They were to **lay aside every weight.** Like casting aside clothes they were to be rid of excessive weights. Greek runners ran almost naked. The word for "weight" *(ogkon)* was used by Galen for bulk of body. They must have no excess fat, must be trained down to their best running weight. This word was also used for arrogant bearing. They must not be overconfident. It might refer to any burdensome load. All of these ideas apply here. One may see in this phrase *ogkon panta* every single thing that would hinder their successful running: fleshly indulgence, lack of faith, lack of dedication, inordinate pride, and laziness.

Furthermore, they were to lay aside "the easily besetting sin." The picture is that of something like a long garment which would wrap around one's legs to prevent successful running. Since the author used **the sin** he was thinking about one particular sin. In the light of preceding discussions it seems to be the sin of failing to fit into God's redemptive purpose. It could include inactivity (cf. 2:1), lack of faith and rebellion (cf. 3:12; 6:6), and attachment to the world and its evils (cf. 10:26 ff.). It could all be summed up in "no faith" *(apistia).* Unlike those who had achieved "by faith" they were in danger of losing their opportunity in God's purpose due to no faith in God to enable them to run the race successfully.

Having made all necessary preparation, the author and readers were to make the effort to **run with patience the race that is set before us.** "Through patience" *(di' hupomonēs)* is in the emphatic position. Regardless of what others might do to them they were to possess the reserve strength necessary to go on to victory. They were not to give up but to run the race completely and successfully.

The race refers to a particular one. Literally, it is "the being set before us race" or *agōna.* This word *agōna* expresses the idea of a contest involving both peril and strain. Seeing this race in terms of the **witnesses** it appears as a relay race. Those witnesses had successfully run their segment of the race. Now they were watching eagerly to see how this generation of God's people would run theirs. For ultimate success in God's world-mission depended upon how well the latest or last segment would be run.

Looking unto Jesus the author and finisher of our faith; who for the joy that was set before him endured the cross, despising the shame, and is set down at the right hand of the throne of God (v.2).

The runners were conscious of the "witnesses." But they really ran for Jesus. An athlete is not to be simply a crowd pleaser; he is to perform so as to receive the commendation of his coach. In this case the coach is Jesus. But he is more. He is the supreme *witness.* He witnessed in his own role in God's redemptive purpose that God can enable one to be faithful and triumphant. He is the **author** (*archēgon,* pioneer, leader) and **finisher** (*teleiōtēn,* goal) of faith. This word *teleiōtēn* is not found in any previous Greek writing. It was probably coined from *teleioō* by the author to express an idea. Jesus is not only the one who pioneered, went before his people, in faith with respect to God's redemptive purpose. He is also the one who is its goal. And he enables those who strive in faith to be victorious (cf. Phil. 4:13).

The **joy** set before Jesus was that of the work of redemption which he accomplished through the sacrifice of himself. He weighed the joy over against the suffering, and found that the former far exceeded the latter (cf. Rom. 8:18). **Endured** renders an aorist form of *hupomenō,* whence comes the word *hupomonē* (cf. v.1). He took all that evil could throw against him, yet possessed strength sufficient to enable him to countercharge to victory.

Crucifixion was the most painful and shameful of deaths. It was reserved only for the worst of criminals (cf. Luke 22:37). Jesus probably was crucified naked. Roman law forbade crucifixion for a Roman citizen. Hence, Jesus, a Roman subject, was crucified, but Paul, a Roman citizen, was beheaded. In order to be man's redeemer Jesus endured the cross and counted as nothing its shame.

Following his resurrection and ascension he "has sat down" (perfect tense of permanency) **at the right hand of the throne of God,** the place of power and glory (cf. Phil. 2:5–11). Note the change from the aorist ("endured") to the perfect tense **(is set down).** Jesus endured the cross *one time.* His sitting down speaks of the permanent effect of his redemptive work.

These Hebrew Christians were to keep their eyes on Jesus as evidence that he could enable them to run the race successfully and receive the reward and glory of victory. It is when God's people take their eyes off Jesus and his will that they falter and fail in God's redemptive mission. Conversely, when they fix their eyes on him they are diligent and triumphant in it.

For consider him that endured such contradiction of sinners against himself, lest ye be wearied and faint in your minds (v.3).

The readers were commanded (imperative) to **consider** Jesus. This verb renders *analogizomai* (note "analyze") and means to compare, reckon up, to weigh. It means to estimate carefully one object in relation to another. Here the verb "endured" (cf. v.2) is a perfect participle. Jesus completely endured the "gainsaying" or talking against himself of sinners. Such gainsaying is the beginning of every act of rebellion. Jesus' enemies opposed him in words before their final act of rebellion seen at the cross.

A textual problem occurs at this point. Some strong manuscripts read **himself** *(heauton),* while others read "themselves" *(heautous).* If the latter be followed it means that they talked and acted against themselves or their own best interests. If the former be followed it means that they did these things against Jesus.

Westcott cites Numbers 16:38 ("sinners against their own souls" or "selves") in connection with the latter reading. This could make sense, the thought being that to rebel against God's will is to sin against one's own self-interest. However, in the context of Hebrews 12:3 the idea more likely is that Jesus' enemies spoke against him. They sinned against themselves in so doing. But their gainsaying was with respect to Jesus.

The reason for their considering or analyzing Jesus is in order that the readers shall not be weary and made feeble in their "souls" *(psuchais)* or "lives." The thought suggests that they shall not be so affected with respect to the purpose of their being as Christians. If their Leader has deported himself so well so can they. Their afflictions and trials are not so great as were his. So they should not be less dedicated in their part of God's world-mission.

2. The Chastening of the Lord (12:4–11)

Jesus shed his blood in order to fulfil his redemptive mission. But, said the author, **Ye have not yet resisted unto blood, striving against sin** (v.4). **Resisted** renders a word meaning to stand against something. It was used of troops lined up in battle against an enemy. They had not yet stood against those who persecuted them "up to [*mechris*] blood" or to the point of dying as they strove **against** or "face to face with sin." "Not yet up to blood" comes first in the sentence, so is emphatic. *Not yet,* but they may be called on to do so. Evidently they were not of Palestine. For some of that number had died for the faith (cf. Stephen and James the apostle, Acts 7:60; 12:2). Even so, these readers were deterred from their place in God's mission because of persecution. How should they regard these trials?

And ye have forgotten the exhortation which speaketh unto you as unto children, My son, despise not thou the chastening of the Lord, nor faint when thou art rebuked of him: for whom the Lord loveth he chasteneth, and scourgeth every son whom he receiveth (vv. 5–6). This statement could be either interrogative or declarative. But since there is no question mark in the Greek text (;), it must be the latter. The author recalled to his readers Proverbs 3:11–12 to help them to understand the purpose of their trials. God did not necessarily send persecution upon them, but if they view it correctly it can be a chastening.

Chastening renders a word *paideias* which comes from *paideuō,* to train a child. So their trials may become, not a cause for rebellion against God, but a means of training them as his children for their world-mission. For this reason they should not **despise** or belittle these experiences. Rather they should see them as a discipline for service.

The Lord trains as children those whom he loves. He scourges or whips them when they disobey. This may be by God's permissive or by his punitive will. Each experience must be viewed in its own context. It is a difficult lesson for children to learn. But it is evidence of maturity when they do.

If ye endure chastening, God dealeth with you as with sons; for what son is he whom the father chasteneth not? But if ye be without chastisement, whereof all are partakers, then are ye bastards, and not sons (vv. 7–8).

The very fact of this training as a child proves their sonship. Such is a father's duty. Freedom from such only shows that one is not a son but a bastard or illegitimate child. Christians often wonder why they suffer when non-Christians at times seem to escape such. This is the reason. A father does not chasten another's son. God not only cares for his own, but his very care causes him to chasten his children in love.

Furthermore we have fathers of our flesh which corrected [chastened] us and we gave them reverence: shall we not much rather be in subjection unto the Father of spirits, and live? (v.9).

The contrast here is between "fathers of the flesh" and "the Father of our spirits." Men do not rebel against the chastening of the former. Rather they reverence or turn to them in obedience. Should not Christians all the more be submissive to God when he does the same? It is by doing so that Christians shall **live.** This verb translates *zaō*. It is used of spiritual life. Here it means to exercise the functions related to spiritual life. It suggests living in accord with God's purpose.

For they verily for a few days chastened us after their own pleasure; but he for our profit, that we might be partakers of his holiness (v.10).

Earthly parents train their children in a manner as seems good to them, **but he [God] for our profit. Profit** means to bear together or to bring together one's powers for proper usage. It is to the end that Christians may be sharers of God's **holiness** which basically means God's separation from mundane things. His people should also be set apart from such to be servants of God.

Now no chastening for the present seemeth to be joyous, but grievous: nevertheless afterward it yieldeth the peaceable fruit of righteousness unto them that are exercised thereby (v.11). This is true in both natural and spiritual experience. The training (chastening) of a child at the moment is not joyous but grievous. The fruits of such are not readily apparent. Yet when seen in the larger picture it yields the peaceable righteousness or that which is in obedience to God's will.

This fruit is to those who **are exercised** to that end. This verb translates the verb *gumnazō* whence comes the English word "gymnasium." At the moment it is not joyous but hard work. However, it becomes joyous in retrospect as the athlete sees that thereby he was prepared to win the victory in the contest. The verb form is a perfect passive participle, expressing the completeness of training.

This figure climaxed the author's figure of training a child. In their present trials the readers were being trained as God's children for their place in God's relay race of his world-mission in redemption. If they properly respond to this "gymnasium" experience, they will be able to be victorious in their segment of this race. One is a victorious Christian who can turn every trying experience into a means of glorifying God in triumphant service for him.

3. The Fellowship of Concern (12:12–17)

Because of this these Hebrew Christians were exhorted to have a mutual concern for each other in their trials. No Christian should live in isolation but should be a part of the *fellowship* that he might strengthen others and be strengthened by them. God's world-mission calls for cooperative service on the part of his people; a concerned fellowship is in itself a strong witness.

Wherefore lift up the hands which hang down, and the feeble knees; and make straight paths for your feet, lest that which is lame be turned out of the way; but let it rather be healed (vv. 12–13).

In this passage the author borrowed phrases from the Old Testament to exhort his readers. (Cf. Isa. 35:3; Deut. 32:36; 2 Sam. 4:1; Psalm 20:8.) **Wherefore** refers back to the arduous but beneficial experience of training. **Lift up** means to make straight or to set right. **Hands which hang down** are relaxed hands. The perfect tense of *pariēmi* means completely relaxed or idle (cf. "left undone" in Luke 11:42). **Feeble knees** are palsied or paralyzed knees (cf. Luke 5:18,24). These figures are significant with regard to those who must either strive in games or in battle. Hands are used in the conflict, and knees are used in making progress such are marching or running.

Furthermore, in the race they were exhorted to **make straight paths for your feet** (cf. Prov. 4:26 f.). This to the end that the feeble knees may not be turned out of joint. Each Christian should help others in order that rather than making one's weakness worse, it may be healed so that he can run his race completely and victoriously. In helping one another, each helps himself. Teamwork is necessary in winning victories in battle, on the athletic field, and in the Lord's work. Therefore—

Follow peace with all men, and holiness, without which no man shall see the Lord: looking diligently lest any man fail of the grace of God; lest any root of bitterness springing up trouble you, and thereby many be defiled (vv. 14–15).

Christians should "chase after peace" as in a hunt. **All** *(pantōn)* is inclusive; it includes the non-Christian as well as the Christian. Without this one's witness for Christ is hindered if not destroyed altogether. A fighting church or denomination is a denial before the world of all that for which the name of Christ stands. If Christ's people cannot live in peace among themselves, who can? (cf. Matt. 5:9). But if they live in peace among themselves, the world will recognize them as sons of God and will want the same relationship. Being at peace with lost people does not mean compromise with their evil deeds. But Christians should love them despite their sins, even as God in Christ does (cf. Rom. 5:8).

Furthermore, Christians should chase after **holiness** *(hagiasmon)*. This means consecration or a state of being set apart to God's work. The definite article *(ton hagiasmon)* refers this to a particular type of consecration, their role in God's world-mission.

Thomas outlines 12:12–17 as (1) our duty to ourselves (vv. 12–15), (2) our duty to others (vv. 13–15), and (3) our duty to God (vv. 14–17).[1]

The author said that apart from "holiness" no one **shall see** God. It should be recalled that the moment one is regenerated he is sanctified or set apart to God's service. Thereafter, he is to develop and serve in that state. Unless one is in that state he shall not see God or appear before him as his child (cf. Matt. 5:8). If one is in this state he should grow and serve in it. The Christian's life should be characterized by unadulterated love and loyalty to God.[2]

This mutual care should lead all Christians to be **looking diligently** upon one another. The verb form is a present participle, "keeping on having oversight" of each other. The root verb is *episkopeō*, to have oversight. From it comes the word *episkopos*, one who oversees the work of others to see that they do their work correctly. (Cf. *bishop, episcopal.*)

So each Christian should keep a watchful eye on others to detect any tendency to rebel against God's will. He is to do so **lest any man fail of the grace of God. Fail** renders a present participle of *hustereō* (cf. 4:1). This does not mean a loss of redemption but that, like Israel at Kadesh-barnea, one shall fall short of God's purpose of grace for all men. God wills to save all men. His purpose in grace involves the witnessing of the redeemed to the unredeemed. So the point is not to keep the redeemed from losing that state, but to fail to be used in that state to share the gospel with a lost world.

The **root of bitterness** refers to Deuteronomy 29:18. The warning is against idolatry. Failure to be active in God's world-mission opens the door for worship of the things of the world, which can defile or taint the entire church fellowship. One such worldly Christian can negate the witness of many faithful ones. And like a plague it can spread through a church fellowship if allowed to go unhindered.

Lest there be any fornicator, or profane person, as Esau, who for one morsel of meat sold his birthright (v.16). This is an obvious reference to Genesis 25: 31–34. The Scripture does not indicate that Esau was a fornicator. But the rabbinic tradition and Philo picture him as a sensualist.[3] Certainly the biblical picture of him is that of a **profane** person. This renders a word meaning "unhallowed." He was not consecrated to God's purpose but to the gratification of his fleshly desires. He sold his birthright for one meal.

Esau, though a twin, was the first-born son of Isaac. According to custom the family line should have run through him. This means that he should have been the one through whom God's redemptive purpose would have been carried forward in his generation. But because of physical desires he considered this as something to be trodden under foot. He despised his place in God's purpose. Therefore, God rejected him and chose Jacob as the one to use (cf. Rom. 9:13; "hate" and "love" refer to choice).

There should not be among these Hebrew Christians, or any other group of believers, an attitude that for physical ease, gratification, or safety would lead one to rebel against God's world-mission. No "Esau" should sell-out the cause of Christ.

For ye know how that afterward, when he would have inherited the blessing, he was rejected: for he found no place of repentance, though he sought it carefully with tears (v.17).

Carefully is not in the best texts. This verse refers back to Genesis 27:30–40. The point here is not how Jacob contrived to get the blessing of Isaac. It is that despite his bargain to sell his birthright, Esau wanted to go back on his bargain. He sought to regain the birthright **with tears** (cf. Gen. 27:34), but it was too late.

It had already been given to another, to Jacob (Israel).

So Esau, no matter how much he regretted his bargain, **found no place for repentance,** or change of heart and attitude. The truth of the matter is that Esau had experienced no such change. He regretted losing his birthright for what it cost him. For under a similar circumstance he probably would have sold it again for physical satisfaction. God could not trust him with so great a responsibility.

This is suggestive of Hebrews 6:4–6. Like Israel at Kadesh-barnea, Esau had lost his opportunity in God's redemptive mission. He continued to be Isaac's son. But he lost his place in God's plan.

This can happen to an individual Christian, a church, or a given segment of God's people in a given point of history. Not a loss of relationship with God, but a loss of opportunity in God's purpose. God can entrust his work only to those who appreciate its importance and who will pay the price in consecration and self-denial to fulfil their part in it.

4. The Greater Incentive (12:18–27)

The author reminded his readers of their greater obligation in God's purpose by comparing the mountain of the old covenant with that of the new covenant. The word for "mount" *(orei)* does not appear in verse 18. But it is understood from the uses of it in verses 20,22. Verses 18–21 refer to Mount Sinai where God gave the law to Moses (cf. Ex. 19:9–13; Deut. 4:11–13). The old covenant was characterized by fear and the inapproachable nature of God.

However, the new covenant was quite different. The figures which follow in verses 22–24 clearly show this.

But ye are come unto mount Sion, and unto the city of the living God, the heavenly Jerusalem, and to an innumerable company of angels, to the general assembly and church of the firstborn, which are written in heaven, and to God the Judge of all, and to the spirits of just men made perfect, and to Jesus the mediator of the new covenant, and to the blood of sprinkling, that speaketh better things than that of Abel (vv. 22–24).

But marks the contrast between verses 18–21 and verses 22–24. Rather than coming to Mount Sinai these readers had come to Mount Zion. This refers to Jerusalem. But the author hastened to show that he was thinking not of the earthly city but of the **heavenly Jerusalem.** Actually he was thinking of a spiritual mountain and city.

This symbolizes God's dwelling with his people (cf. Rev. 21:1–3,22; 22:3 f.). At Sinai God only passed by in one moment of majesty; here he dwells with his people.

The city to which Christians have come is populated with certain ones. First, there is the **innumerable company of angels** or "myriads of angels." The Jews thought that God gave the law to Moses through angels. But here all angels are gathered "in festal assembly." The word rendered **general assembly** *(panēgurei)* is used in verb form *(panēgurizo)* in Isaiah 66:10 for keeping a festive holiday. Whereas angels at Sinai were associated with the fearful scene of giving the law, here they are seen in a picture of gladness and rejoicing.

What is the occasion of this festal assembly? In view of the author's custom of drawing his figures from the Old Testament, one is justified to view it in terms of Isaiah 66. This chapter describes the messianic kingdom. In verses 7–9 Isaiah shows how God's redemptive purpose will be accomplished. It is then that the prophet calls on his readers to rejoice and be glad with Jerusalem. While in his context of history one may see the earthly Jerusalem, it points beyond it to the heavenly Jerusalem of the messianic kingdom.

May one not also see in this festal assembly the triumphant entry of Jesus into his capital city following his victory over sin and death (cf. Eph. 4:8–12)? And, of course, one is reminded of Luke 15:7,10. The picture in Hebrews 12:22 f. is that of a festal assembly of angels celebrating the completion of Jesus' redemptive work and the fruits of it.

Second, there is the **church of the firstborn.** Interpreters see a problem in the relation of *panēgurei.* Does it relate to "angels" or "the church of the firstborn"? Probably the former. But it colors the latter also. **Firstborn** is used to refer to Israel as God's people (Ex. 4:22). As it is used here it is related to the "church" in the sense of all the redeemed of all the ages, or to the true Israel of God. So these also are a part of this festal assembly (cf. Rev. 5:11–14).

Note that those of this church **are written in heaven** or enrolled there. The verb is a perfect passive participle of *apographō,* the intensive form of the verb "to write." The names of the redeemed are written or enrolled in heaven by God as a finished work. They will stand written. So this alone denies apostasy (cf. Rev. 20:15). The perfect form of *graphō* is also used in Revelation 20:15.

Third, they came **to God the Judge of all.** As God created all men, so is he their Judge. This suggests that the readers will one day face him as Judge. The final judgment will not determine whether one is redeemed or lost. It will only reveal one's condition. But this will be a judgment as to degrees of reward and punishment (cf. Luke 12:47 f.; also Matt. 25:14–46). This alone should provide incentive for the redeemed and sanctified to be faithful in that state, looking toward glorification when they stand before God in Christ at the final judgment.

Fourth, the scene includes **the spirits of just men made perfect.** This group includes the justified ones who have fulfilled their reason for being as the people of God. Looking to the final consummation of the age it means that the faithfulness of the saints in God's redemptive mission has reached its complete accomplishment (perfect participle, cf. 11:40).

Fifth, the scene includes **Jesus the mediator of the new covenant.** Note "Jesus," not Christ (cf. Phil. 2:10 f.). He is there in his deity-humanity. The word for **new** is *neas,* not *kainēs.* Moffatt sees these as synonyms in the Koine Greek.[4] But Dods notes that the classical distinction between the words is preserved here.[5] He says that the author wanted to stress that it was "the recent covenant (*neas* 'new in time,' not as usual, *kainēs* 'fresh in quality,') because the idea first in the writer's mind is not the opposition to the old but the recent origin of the new."

Sixth, those coming to the heavenly Jerusalem see **the blood of sprinkling.** This sprinkling refers back to Hebrews 9:19–28. Moses sealed the old covenant with animal blood (Ex. 24:8). Christ sealed the new covenant in his own blood. And even though Abel's sacrifice still speaks to men (cf. 11:4), it has no message comparable to that of Jesus.

The purpose of the author in making this comparison (vv. 18–24) is to show the greater incentive for faithfulness in God's world-mission under the new covenant than the Israelites had under the old. This is clearly stated in verses 25–27.

See that ye refuse not him that speaketh. For if they escaped not who refused him that spake on earth, much more shall not we escape, if we turn away from him that speaketh from heaven (v.25).

See *(blepete)* may be recognized as an earnest warning. It is also rendered "take heed" in 3:12. In both instances it may be rendered "beware!" The author was driving home the entire lesson of the epistle.

Refuse renders *paraiteomai.* Basically it means to beg or ask. In Hebrews 12:19 it is translated "entreated." The Israelites asked God to stop speaking to them through Moses at Sinai. However, a resultant meaning when used with the accusative of a person, as in 12:25, is to decline to hear someone in the sense of disobedience.[6]

So the readers are warned not to shut their ears, hearts, and wills to the call of God. The Israelites asked God to cease speaking at Sinai. They refused to hear God on earth, particularly at Kadesh-barnea, and they lost their opportunity in God's purpose. They lived and died in a wilderness of regret. But how much greater will be the penalty to the readers who rebel against God's spoken will when he speaks from heaven and about heavenly things. This argument from the lesser to the greater runs throughout the epistle.

Whose voice then shook the earth: but now he hath promised, saying, Yet once more I shake not the earth only, but also heaven (v.26).

The earth shook at Sinai at the voice of God (cf. v.25). But he has promised (perfect tense, a promise that continues) again. The author quoted Haggai 2:6. Verse 7 was related to the coming of the Christ, "the desire of all nations." This could refer to the first coming of Christ, for that coming did **shake** (*seisō,* shake as an earthquake, cf. "seismograph"). But in the context of Hebrews 12:26 the reference is to the second coming of Christ. **Yet once more** gives it this meaning.

And this word, Yet once more, signifieth the removing of those things that are shaken, as of things that are made, that those things which cannot be shaken may remain (v.27).

The author explained **yet once more** in terms of the final testing of all things. It is akin to Paul's trial by fire in 1 Corinthians 3:12–15. The transient things of the world will not abide this shaking, only the permanent things related to God's eternal purpose.

The inference is that Christians should invest their time, talents, and energy, not in worldly, temporal things, but in the abiding things of God's redemptive purpose. Jesus said the same thing in Matthew 6:19–21. Rather than to lay up perishable treasures on earth, they should lay up imperishable treasures in heaven.

Many years ago President Pat Neff of Baylor University commented on laying up treasures in heaven. He said that preachers had been telling him to do this, but that no one had told him how to get his treasures into heaven. He concluded that to do this one must invest his earthly treasures in things that are going to heaven. Not cattle, land, stocks, bonds, oil, or other earthly things—but in men, women, boys, and girls.

Christians should invest not only their money but also their lives in preparing them to go to heaven. This was the point which Jesus made in the parable of the shrewd steward (cf. Luke 16:1 ff.). He concluded, "Make to yourselves friends of the mammon of unrighteousness; that, when ye [it] fail[s], they may receive you into everlasting habitations" (v.9). Earthly treasures will fail. They should be used so as to point "friends" to heaven. Then when a person arrives there, he will be welcomed by those who have preceded him and who are there by virtue of the proper use of his earthly opportunities.

This is the climax of the author's argument about incentives. There can be no better investment on the part of a Christian's life than to give himself and what he possesses as a stewardship to the cause of God's world-mission.

5. The Greater Obligation (12:28–29)

With a final challenge the author concluded this section of his argument before going on to personal matters within the church to which he was writing.

Wherefore we receiving a kingdom which cannot be moved, let us have grace, whereby we may serve God acceptably with reverence and godly fear (v.28).

This is the third **wherefore** *(dio)* in this chapter. The author used it nine times in the epistle (3:7,10; 6:1; 10:5; 11:12,16; 12:12,28; 13:12). In chapter 12, verse 1 encompasses chapter 11 (secondarily 1:1—11:40). Verse 12 draws from 12:1–11. Verse 28 may well be regarded as referring primarily to verses 25–27, but in a very real sense it encompasses all of the epistle up to this point.

Having an unshakeable kingdom, the author and his readers should "keep on having grace" (present tense). This is the grace of responsibility and opportunity by which to serve God in his world-mission (cf. Rom. 12:3; 15:15 f.; Gal. 2:9; Eph. 3:8). They are to **serve** *(latreuōmen)* as priests or a priest-people in a manner that will be "well pleasing" (acceptable) to God. And they are to do so **with reverence and godly fear.**

Godly fear *(deous)* is a word which expresses an apprehension of danger as in a forest. Vincent says that "when the voice and tread of a wild beast are distinctly heard close at hand the *deos* becomes *phobos* [fear]." [7]

It is with such apprehension that Christians should serve God. The apprehension is that they may fail God in his world-mission. The readers of this epistle had not yet failed, but were in danger of doing so. Therefore, their *deos* should become *phobos* lest the apprehension become a reality.

For our God is a consuming fire (v.29). This is taken from Deuteronomy 4:24. Moses was speaking to the generation following the one which rebelled at Kadesh-barnea. He himself would not go into Canaan, but these Israelites led by Joshua would. They would enter into the Canaan "rest" (*katapausis,* cf. 4:3). But if they succumbed to idolatry they would fail in their sabbath-kind-of-rest (*sabbatismos,* cf. 4:9). Future history revealed that even after entering Canaan, Israel failed to fulfil her place in God's world-mission for this very reason.

So Moses said, "Take heed unto yourselves, lest ye forget the covenant of the Lord your God, which he made with you [cf. Ex. 19], and make you a graven image, or the likeness of any thing, which the Lord thy God hath forbidden [cf. Ex. 20:4 ff.]. For the Lord thy God is a consuming fire, even a jealous God" (Deut. 4:23 f.).

Against this background the author warned his readers never to falter in their new covenant relation with God. They too were a priest-nation. Like the generation to which Moses spoke, they could be turned away from fulfilling their spiritual destiny by being wedded to the idols of materialism and worldly aims and ambitions.

It is at this point that present-day Christians are largely failing in their portion of God's world-mission. World conditions may be largely traced to such a failure. The Christian gospel is the only message that can meet the deepest needs of men's hearts. God is depending upon his people to declare it. If they fail him by refusing to hear his call, they shall lose their opportunity and, in the process, may see the world go up in nuclear flames.

But God's purpose will not fail. If the Lord delays his coming, God will choose another generation of his people to do his bidding. Even if the world goes on in its stumbling way, spared from a holocaust by the mercy of God, those Christian groups which refuse to hear and obey will lose their opportunity. Then God will choose others. Even now there is evidence that the center of Christian growth and power is shifting from the larger, more established groups to other groups on fire with zeal for God's world-mission.

Those groups, churches, and individuals who turn a deaf ear to God's call to a world-mission should beware. "For our God is a consuming fire" (v.29; cf. 10:31). He burns up that which cannot stand the trial by fire.

Notes

1. *Op. cit.,* pp. 162 f.; cf. Manson, *op. cit.,* p. 85
2. Cf. Archer, *op. cit.,* p. 91.
3. Cf. Grant, *op. cit.,* p. 56.
4. *Op. cit.,* p. 218
5. *Op. cit.,* p. 373
6. Arndt and Gingrich, *Op. cit.,* p. 621
7. Cf. Robertson, *Op. cit.,* p. 443

XIII. The Need for Christian Fellowship

Christians must be bound together in fellowship if they are to live their lives to the maximum for Christ. Thus, God provided churches wherein his people might be bound together in spiritual bonds. The Greek word for this relationship is *koinōnia,* fellowship. It means a sharing. The word itself is used in 13:16 in the sense of "communicate." However, the idea is present throughout this chapter in the sense of sharing both in the privileges and responsibilities inherent in such a relationship. This was necessary if this group of Christians, or any other, was to fulfil its role in God's purpose.

Thus in his closing remarks the author touched upon certain matters involved in Christian fellowship. The first twelve chapters form a complete work. But in the final one the author dealt with certain personal matters. It should be recalled that someone said that Hebrews begins like an essay, proceeds like a sermon, and ends like a letter. Chapter 13 is the *letter.* However, even in it the author with fresh vigor carried through the theme so evident in the body of the epistle: that certain things are necessary if the readers were to fulfil their place in God's world-mission.

1. The Fellowship of Love (13:1-3)

Let brotherly love continue (v.1). Literally, "the brotherly love, let it continue" or "abide." The word rendered **brotherly love** is *philadelphia.* It is a compound word made up of *philia,* warm, friendly love, and *adelphos,* brother. *Adelphos* is akin to another word which means "out of the same womb." Since these Hebrew Christians had the same source of spiritual life (God in Christ), they should love each other as brothers. It should be an abiding relationship.

Such a relationship within itself is a witness for Christ to a lost world. An early Roman writer commented on how Christians loved each other. It was in response to the Lord's teachings (cf. John 15:12). The fact that these Christians lived in a hostile social and spiritual environment made this "love of the brethren" all the more necessary.

Be not forgetful to entertain strangers: for thereby some have entertained angels unawares (v.2). The public accommodations for travellers were few and far between. Even where available they were hardly suitable. So this admonition was a needed one. This hospitality was probably directed toward fellow-Christians who travelled. If the readers lived in Rome this would be all the more meaningful. For doubtless many such came to Rome (cf. Rom. 16:1 f.). Some of these would be Christian witnesses like Paul.

Be not forgetful renders a present imperative verb preceded by the negative particle *mē*. It may read "stop being forgetful." Apparently they had not been hospitable enough. The word rendered **entertain strangers** is *philoxenias*. Like *philadelphia* it also means "love for strangers." The word was used in the sense of hospitality (cf. Rom. 12:13).

Referring back to the case of Abraham (Gen. 18) the author reminded his readers that in showing hospitality to strangers **some have entertained angels unawares.** A careful reading of Genesis 18 shows that unknowingly Abraham had the Lord himself as a guest. And did not Jesus say that in being kind to his own, one is showing kindness to him (cf. Matt. 25:40,45; John 13:20)?

Remember them that are in bonds, as bound with them; and them which suffer adversity, as being yourselves also in the body (v.3).

Fellow-Christians perhaps were in bonds for their faith. So the readers were commanded to be mindful of them and their needs. They were to do so as if they also were in bonds with them. Others were free but suffered ill treatment. They should be mindful of them as though they were in the bodies of those who so suffered.

So close should be their fellowship that when one suffered all suffered. This reads as though they were aware of Paul's words in 1 Corinthians 12. Certainly such a response would be the Golden Rule in action (cf. Matt. 7:12; Acts 4:32–37). So intricately bound to Christ were his people that to persecute them was to persecute him (Acts 9:4). What a wonderful thing it would be if all Christians so regarded themselves in their relationship to other Christians (cf. 1 Cor. 12:26)!

2. The Fellowship of Conduct (13:4–8)

Not only should all Christians suffer when one suffers, but all Christians are either honored or shamed when one is honored or shamed. So all Christians should so conduct themselves as to bring honor to Christ and his *body.*

Marriage is honorable in all, and the bed undefiled: but whoremongers and adulterers God will judge (v.4).

In the Greek text there is no verb in the former part of this verse. It must be supplied. And it may simply be declarative, "Marriage is [*estin*] honorable." Or it may be a command: "Let marriage be [*estō*] honorable." **In all** means in all respects or circumstances. The verb should also be read in connection with **the bed undefiled.** "To defile the bed" was a common expression for adultery (Robertson). When taken in the context of the entire verse, the sense seems to be a command. This is seen in the word "for" *(gar)* in the latter half of the verse, as showing that God judges fornicators and adulterers. So it perhaps should read, "Let marriage be honorable in all respects, and let the bed be undefiled: for God will judge fornicators and adulterers."

Let your conversation be without covetousness; and be content with such things as ye have: for he hath said, I will never leave thee, nor forsake thee (v.5).

The verb *estō* should also be used here. **Conversation** translates *ho tropos* meaning "way." Here it is the way one lives. **Without covetousness** renders one word *aphilarguros.* This is a word meaning "a lover of money" with the *alpha privative* which reverses the meaning of the word. Or "not a lover of money." "Let your manner of life be without love of money." Instead of being a lover of money they should be lovers of the brethren and of strangers (cf. vv. 1–2).

Love of money could lead to dishonesty. The love of money honestly obtained could dry up humankindness and missionary zeal in miserly hearts. So one should be satisfied with what he has (cf. Phil. 4:11–13).

To reinforce this admonition the author quoted what Robertson calls "a free paraphrase" ("a popular paraphrase," Moffatt) of Genesis 28:15; Deuteronomy 31:8; Joshua 1:5; I Chronicles 28:20. Philo used these very words. But Westcott questions that the author borrowed them from him. Rather he suggests that the words drawn from these cited passages had become a commonly used saying.[1]

I will never leave thee, nor forsake thee. The verb rendered **leave** means to abandon *(aniēmi).* "Forsake" *(egkataleipō)* also means to abandon, desert, or leave alone in the field of contest, or in a condition of suffering. Jesus used this word on the cross (Matt. 27:46). In common parlance it may be expressed as to leave in the lurch. This is a strong negative statement. It contains five negative particles, two double negatives *ou me* (in the emphatic position) and *oudi.* Literally, "Not never you I will abandon, neither not never you I will forsake." There could be no stronger statement of this—two strong negative statements as a parallelism or repeated for emphasis.

It is of interest to note that all the cited passages for this saying have to do with someone who had a service to perform for God. And He promised to be with them in it. Two of these had to do with Joshua who led Israel into Canaan: at his appointment (Deut. 31:8), and as he was about to lead the nation into the land of promise. Westcott notes that "the position of the Jewish Christians corresponded spiritually with that of their fathers on the verge of Canaan." [2] So this relates the promise to the Exodus epic. Therefore, this promise apparently was related by the author to his readers as they faced their world-mission. God not only can supply for their material needs, but can enable them to achieve their spiritual reason for being. So, rather than to pursue material glory and greatness they should pursue their spiritual destiny as a priest-people.

Against this background the author and his readers could say "boldly" or "with good courage," "The Lord is my helper, and I will not fear what man shall do unto me" (v.6; cf. Psalm 118:6). Despite persecution these Hebrew Christians can tackle courageously their God-given task, knowing that God will help them to accomplish it.

Remember them that have the rule over you, who have spoken unto you the word of God: whose faith follow, considering the end of their conversation (v.7).

If the readers were to fulfil their ministry for Christ, they must be mindful of the ones leading them. Some see these as their present church leaders, e.g. pastors and deacons. The participle rendered **them that have the rule** *(hēgoumenōn)* is present tense. However, it may read "the ones leading from time to time." This plus the aorist form "have spoken" *(elalēsan)* would make these to be former leaders. It could be those who had founded the church. Robertson even includes the heroes in chapter 11. In the light of *pistin,* faith, this is entirely possible. These by their faithful performance in the past, plus those who more recently had preached **the word of God** to them, were worthy of being remembered. "The word of God" was used to refer to both the Old Testament and the Christian revelation. Perhaps the major emphasis was upon the latter as it showed the fulfilment in Christ of God's redemptive purpose.

They were exhorted to imitate *(mimeisthe)* the faith of both the heroes of faith and the more recent leaders, as they carefully observed the issue (things going out) of their manner of life. The heroes had proved the value of faith in accomplishing for God. The readers themselves were the fruit of faithfulness to the world-mission on the part of others.

Jesus Christ the same yesterday, and to-day, and for ever (v.8).

The verb "is," though not in the Greek text, probably should be inserted after "Christ." At first glance this may seem to be a great truth not necessarily related to the context. But was not the author saying that as Jesus Christ had himself brought victory in God's redemptive purpose, so He could give victory to those who follow him in it?

Yesterday could include both his role in God's redemptive purpose in eternity and in history. He is able to give victory **today** at the time the readers faced their own crisis with respect to God's world-mission, and he can do so "unto the ages." Robertson notes that this means eternity as well as the Greek can say it. There was no reason, therefore, why these Hebrew Christians should not launch out into the full stream of God's redemptive will and purpose.

3. The Fellowship of Faith (13:9–16)

If God's people are to witness effectively for Christ they must have a firmly fixed faith in him. Otherwise the gospel trumpet will give an uncertain sound. One of the greatest obstacles to Christian missions and evangelism is at this very point.

Be not carried about with divers and strange doctrines. For it is a good thing that the heart be established with grace; not with meats, which have not profited them that have been occupied therein (v.9).

The many-colored and unheard-of teachings apparently refer to Jewish incursions into the Christian community. This is suggested by **meats** or dietary laws. Christians are not under law but under grace. Paul had to contend with this problem repeatedly.

That it was a present and urgent problem is seen in the present passive imperative verb preceded by the negative particle *mē.* It could read **be not carried about** or "stop being carried about" or away as though it were already going on. Such had produced a doctrinal crisis in the church. And a church absorbed in doctrinal debate will hardly be devoted to declaring the gospel to a lost world.

The author declared that it is good for the heart to be stabilized by grace. Evidently the Jewish teachers were saying that spiritual security would come from a proper observance of dietary laws. But the author reminded his readers that such rituals had failed to build up these Jews spiritually. Why then should the Hebrew Christians be bound by such unprofitable legalism? Only God's grace in their hearts could suffice for them.

We have an altar, whereof they have no right to eat which serve the tabernacle. For the bodies of those beasts, whose blood is brought into the sanctuary by the high priest for sin, are burned without the camp (vv. 10–11). These verses express a contrast between those under the old covenant and those under the new. Apparently these Jewish teachers had been telling the Christians that since they had no altar of sacrifice they were missing some spiritual blessing.

But the emphatic position of **have** means that "we *have* an altar." It is one from which those who ministered as priests in the tabernacle have no right to eat. The author further mentioned the custom of burning, not eating, the bodies of sacrificial animals on the Day of Atonement (v.11). Under the old covenant the priests were permitted to eat certain portions of sacrifices except those made on the Day of Atonement. The day-to-day sacrifices were made for *sins* committed by the people. But the Day of Atonement sacrifices were for *sin.*

The point of the author is that under the new covenant there is but one altar and sacrifice, the two regarded as one, and that the once-for-all sacrifice of Christ. It fulfilled the Day of Atonement sacrifice, and its thorough cleansing made no longer necessary the day-to-day sacrifices. Since the priests could not eat any portion of the Day of Atonement sacrifice, they had no advantage over the Hebrew Christians in the eating of meats.

Of course, the overall thought is that in Christ's one atoning sacrifice the Hebrew Christians have all that is necessary for cleansing from *sin* and *sins.* It is another example of the superiority of the new covenant over the old.

Wherefore Jesus also, that he might sanctify the people with his own blood, suffered without the gate (v.12).

This corresponds to the thought of burning the sacrifice outside the camp (cf. v.11). Jesus was crucified "outside the gate," a statement which corresponds to "outside the camp" in verse 11 (cf. John 19:17). He did this in order that he might **sanctify** (purge from sin and set apart to God's service) them through **his own blood,** not the blood of animals.

Let us go forth therefore unto him without the camp, bearing his reproach (v.13). Rather than to return to the altar of Judaism with its endless line of sacrifices, the author exhorted his readers to "keep on going out to him" or to Christ (present middle volitive subjunctive). In other words, they should take their stand alongside him.

Evidently the Jewish teachers had been debasing Jesus as one who died not redemptively but as a criminal who received his just punishment. So the Hebrew

Christians were to bear his reproach, the shameful and painful death (cf. 12:2). His reproach was their glory, as indeed it was his. They were not to allow the false teachers to deter them from their purpose in Christ.

For here we have no continuing city, but we seek one to come (v.14).

Since Jerusalem and its temple had no meaning for these Christians, they are pictured as having on earth no abiding city. Like Abraham they look for a heavenly city which has eternal foundations (cf. 11:10). This within itself should hold them to their faith and to God's purpose for them.

By [*dia,* through] **him therefore let us offer the sacrifice of praise to God continually, that is, the fruit of our lips giving thanks to his name** (v.15).

Instead of returning to Jewish altars to offer animal sacrifices, they were called upon to offer continually a sacrifice of praise to God (cf. Lev. 7:12; Psalm 54:6). This sacrifice is "the fruit of lips confessing his name." "Confessing" (giving thanks) may be used in the sense of praise or gratitude. But it may also mean to confess or own Jesus as the Christ and Saviour (cf. Matt. 10:32).

Therefore, this could mean to praise God by remaining true to Jesus and by confessing him before men as God's anointed for salvation. This could involve the missionary note, so God's world-mission. Since Christ had made the one complete sacrifice, the only continuing sacrifice these Hebrew Christians should make is one of praise to God by sharing the effects of this sacrifice with a lost world.

But to do good and to communicate forget not: for with such sacrifices God is well pleased (v.16). Doing good and sharing relate to serving the poor, such as with alms. These things are well pleasing to God. Westcott comments, "Spiritual sacrifice must find an outward expression. Praise to God is service to men." Such would be a demonstration of the faith which the readers professed. As God is gracious to them, so must they be gracious to others.

4. The Fellowship of Mutual Concern (13:17–19)

This mutual concern is with respect both to those who lead in the local church and to the author himself. In both cases it has to do with the work of the Lord.

Obey them that have the rule over you, and submit yourselves: for they watch for [*huper,* on behalf of] **your souls, as they that must give account, that they may do it with joy, and not with grief: for that is unprofitable for you** (v.17).

In verse 7 the author had called on his readers to be mindful of those who had preceded them in the faith, including former leaders and/or the founders of their church. Now he urged them to follow their present leaders. They were to **obey them** and to **submit** to their leadership. Only thus may a given church be effective in the Lord's work. The reason for this dual injunction is that these leaders have a responsibility for which they must give an account to God. **Watch** renders a verb meaning to be watchful, to be sleepless. The present tense means a constant condition. These leaders were going without sleep in their vigil to be watchful on behalf of their **souls** *(tōn psuchōn).* This could also mean the purpose of their lives in Christ. It would be the responsibility of these leaders to enlist, develop, and direct them in their world-mission.

It is a happy church which has such devoted leaders. Happy are those church leaders who enjoy a mutual concern and cooperation on the part of those whom they are charged to lead. Any other relationship leads to grief for the leaders and an unprofitable ministry on the part of the church itself.

Pray for us: for we trust we have a good conscience, in all things willing to live honestly. But I beseech you the rather to do this, that I may be restored to you the sooner (vv. 18–19).

The relationship to the local leaders naturally suggested the readers' wider fellowship with the author and those who worked with him. So he called on this church to pray for them. The author and his companions may have been accused by the Jewish teachers (v.9) of being untrue to their responsibility. The doctrinal crisis could have caused the love of some toward them to grow cold. However, regardless of what had been reported to the church, the author and his co-laborers had a good conscience in the matter and willed to live honorably in every respect.

But the primary reason for his request for prayer was that they might hasten his restoration to them. He longed to be with them personally. Evidently he was not in prison (cf. v.23). This delay may have been due to illness. So he was asking them to pray for his health. One sees in this request a tender note of love between the author and the readers.

5. The Fellowship of Sanctification (13:20–21)

This is one of the most beautiful benedictions found in the Bible. But it is more than that alone. It is a prayer that God will enable the readers to be fully dedicated to his will and purpose. As the author and his companions served the Lord in good conscience, so he prayed that they should do the same.

Now the God of peace, that brought again from the dead our Lord Jesus, that great shepherd of the sheep, through the blood of the everlasting covenant, make you perfect in every good work to do his will, working in you that which is well-pleasing in his sight, through Jesus Christ; to whom be glory for ever and ever. Amen (vv. 20–21).

Only one comment is necessary. "Make perfect" renders a verb (*katartizō*, to equip), which in 10:5 is rendered "prepared." As God equipped the Son with a body in which he might fulfil his part in God's redemptive purpose, so the author prayed that God would also equip them for their part in this purpose. Here then is the world-mission again. So this benediction is not only beautiful; it has a practical aspect as well. As Christ was sanctified to his work so should they be to theirs.

6. The Fellowship of Personal Relations (13:22–25)

Having finished the body of his letter (v.21, "amen"), the author closed with certain personal matters. Westcott calls this section a *postscript*.

And I beseech you, brethren, suffer the word of exhortation: for I have written

a letter unto you in few words (v.22). He asked that they "bear with" the brevity of the letter in the light of the tremendous themes with which he has dealt. It is not an apology for what he has said. Rather he emphasized that despite its brevity the exhortation is important and urgent. Certainly the tone of the epistle, especially the five hortatory passages, shows this to be true.

Know ye that our brother Timothy is set at liberty; with whom, if he come shortly, I will see you (v.23). What imprisonment this was he did not say. But it would be good news to his readers that Timothy had been set free. And added to that was the prospect that soon they would see both him and Timothy.

Salute all them that have the rule over you, and all the saints. They of Italy salute you (v.24). This was a parting greeting to the entire church, including its leaders. In colloquial language it could mean simply, "Say hello to everyone in the church." And "The ones from *(apo)* Italy say hello."

Interpreters differ as to those "of Italy." Some see them as saints *in* Italy sending greetings to a church elsewhere. Others see them as saints *from* Italy sending greetings home to their Christian friends there. The word *apo,* from, seems to favor the latter view. How one regards this affects whether the epistle was written elsewhere to saints in Italy (Rome) or from Italy to a church located elsewhere. This determination does not affect the purpose and meaning of Hebrews.

Grace be with you all (v.25). **Amen** is not in the best texts. The Greek text reads "the grace," so probably a shortened form of "the grace of our Lord Jesus Christ" (cf. 1 Cor. 16:23). The readers would need it if they were to fulfil their place in God's world-mission of redemption.

Notes

1. *Op. cit.,* p. 434.
2. *Op. cit.,* p. 435.

XIV. Conclusion

At the outset various views were noted as to the purpose of Hebrews. Able interpreters hold to one or another of these positions. One's view of the epistle determines how he interprets the overall work, and especially the five exhortations given by the author.

The writer stated his position as seeing the purpose of Hebrews to be a challenge to its readers to go forward in finding and filling their place in God's world-mission of redemption. It is a call to evangelism and missions. It is also a warning as to the consequences of failure in fulfilling one's part in this world-mission.

Such a position avoids the problem of apostasy in the light of strong New Testament teachings to the contrary. Furthermore, it places Hebrews, not in the backwaters of a problem which would have been peculiar only to a church of Hebrew Christians faced with the temptation of forsaking Christ to return to the legal aspects of Judaism, but in the mainstream of God's redemptive purpose for all men. It faces the problem of an arrested development, but goes beyond that to show the goal toward which the people of God should move. And it relates this goal to the present as well as to the final consummation of the age. Scant attention has been paid to the position which sees the readers as Jews contemplating becoming Christians, or to the view that the readers were in danger of leaving their Christian faith to plunge into Gentile pagan practices. The former seems to be negated by the many Christian references made to the readers. The latter seems to be based upon incidentals and to be foreign to the main body of thought in the epistle.

The evidence of the Exodus epic is too strong to be ignored. It places the readers of the epistle in a situation similar to that of their Israelite forebears. To the writer this gives a natural and firm basis upon which to interpret both the comparisons between elements of the old covenant and the superior ones of the new covenant. It also seems to make more intelligible the warnings and exhortations which àre spaced throughout the epistle.

Someone has noted that Hebrews is one of the most neglected books in the New Testament. Is this not due to the fact that traditional interpretations have removed it largely from any relevancy to the present age in Christian history? If the writer's view be a valid one, it makes Hebrews as up-to-date as the latest news headline. It becomes a clarion call to Christian people in every age to launch out upon the stream of God's redemptive world-mission. For only thus can they strike a telling blow for God in turning the world to him who alone is the God of history and who alone has the words of eternal life.

The shame of Christian people in this age, as in previous ones, is that so few of them are ardently giving their witness concerning Christ. Vast bodies of Christendom are only playing at the game of world missions and evangelism. God's people everywhere are in a state of arrested development. When they should be on the firing line for God, multitudes are still in the "nursery" of their churches drinking milk.

The world faces its greatest crisis in history. This generation of God's people stands at its Kadesh-barnea. Will it rebel against God and die in a wilderness of wasted opportunity? Or will it heed the ancient warning and enter into its "rest" that it might carry out its "sabbath-kind-of-rest"?

Bibliography

ARCHER, GLEASON L., JR. *The Epistle to the Hebrews.* Grand Rapids: Baker Book House, 1957.

BARCLAY, WILLIAM. *The Letter to the Hebrews.* Philadelphia: Westminster Press, 1955.

BOWMAN, JOHN WICK. *Hebrews, James, I and II Peter.* ("The Layman's Bible Commentary.") Richmond: John Knox Press, 1962.

COTTON, J. HARRY, and PURDY, ALEXANDER C. "The Epistle to the Hebrews," *The Interpreter's Bible,* Vol. 11. Nashville: Abingdon Press, 1955.

DELITZSCH, FRANZ. *Commentary on the Epistle to the Hebrews.* 2 vols. Grand Rapids: Wm. B. Eerdmans Publishing Co., 1952.

DODS, MARCUS. "The Epistle to the Hebrews," *The Expositor's Greek Testament,* Vol. IV. Grand Rapids: Wm. B. Eerdmans Publishing Co., 1951.

GRANT, FREDERICK C. *The Epistle to the Hebrews.* ("Tyndale Bible Commentary," Vol. 15) Grand Rapids: Wm. B. Eerdmans Publishing Co., 1960.

HOBBS, HERSCHEL H. *Studies in Hebrews.* Nashville: Sunday School Board, SBC, 1954.

IRONSIDE, H. A. *Studies in the Epistle to the Hebrews.* New York: Loiseaux Brothers, 1932.

MANSON, WILLIAM. *The Epistle to the Hebrews.* London: Hodder and Stoughton, 1951.

MOFFATT, JAMES. *The Epistle to the Hebrews.* ("The International Critical Commentary.") Grand Rapids: Wm. B. Eerdmans Publishing Co., 1924.

NEIL, WILLIAM. *The Epistle to the Hebrews.* London: SCM Press, 1955.

REES, T. "Epistle to the Hebrews," *The International Standard Bible Encyclopedia,* Vol. II. Grand Rapids: Wm. B. Eerdmans Publishing Co., 1949.

ROBERTSON, A. T. "Hebrews," *Word Pictures in the New Testament,* Vol. V. Nashville: Broadman Press, 1932.

SCHNEIDER, JOHANNES. *The Letter to the Hebrews.* Grand Rapids: Wm. B. Eerdmans Publishing Co., 1957.

THOMAS, W. H. GRIFFITH. *Let Us Go On.* Grand Rapids: Zondervan Publishing House, 1954.

WESTCOTT, BROOKE FOSS. *The Epistle to the Hebrews.* London: Macmillan, 1928.

WUEST, KENNETH S. *Hebrews in the Greek New Testament.* Grand Rapids: Wm. B. Eerdmans Publishing Co., 1953.